Legal Almanac Series No. 32

THE CRIMES AND PUNISHMENT PRIMER

by B.R. WHITE

General Editor
Irving J. Sloan

1986
Oceana Publications, Inc.
Dobbs Ferry, New York

345.73
W582 cr

Library of Congress Cataloging-in-Publication Data

White, Bertha Rothe.   87-3000
    The crimes and punishment primer.

    (Legal almanac series ; no. 32)
    Includes index.
    1. Criminal law—United States—States—Popular
works.   I. Title.   II. Series.
KF9220.W48   1986   345.73   86-5097
ISBN 0-379-11151-9   347.305

Manufactured in the United States of America

TABLE OF CONTENTS

PREFACE

Criminal law is in essence a means of social control, and grows ever more complex in our complex society. It is as old as the murderer Cain, and as new as the most recent campus riot. Because of the multiplicity of acts of omission and commission punishable as crimes in our fifty states, it is necessary to limit the scope of this book to the major crimes, so as to give a better understanding of them.

Each of the states has its own definitions and penalties for crimes and misdemeanors, and the law varies from one to another. In addition, where the Congress has decreed that some act is a crime and has provided a penalty for it, the federal courts will try the wrongdoer, but under a Supreme Court ruling they will not try any common law crimes not enumerated in federal acts.

Our law originated in the common law of England, which goes back to the ancient times when there were unwritten laws originating in custom and usage. Gradually certain customs came to be adopted as the way to deal with a certain set of facts, either in controversies between men or in misdeeds. Judges considered themselves bound by prior similar cases, so in the later period the common law was fixed by judicial decision, and then by legislation, which restated and added to or changed the common law.

When the colonists came to the United States from England, they brought with them this body of law, statutory and common. Together with the laws enacted in England before the Revolution, this formed the basis of our law in the states, and still governs, except where changed or abolished by individual state legislatures. Louisiana is an exception to this, since it was settled by the French, who used the Civil Law system as it developed on the continent of Europe. But even Louisiana has adopted some common law principles, as may be seen in comparing her criminal statutes in the tables with those of other states.

Because of the similarity of the laws as they developed from the common law basis in the fifty states, criminal laws may be discussed in a general manner.

THE CRIMES AND PUNISHMENT PRIMER

Chapter 1

AN OVERVIEW OF CRIMINAL ACTS

Criminal law has its beginnings in the dim past, when men first began to live together in society. Its purpose is not primarily to detect and punish wrongdoers, but to define socially unacceptable actions, those which violate law and order, cause harm to another person or his property, or are detrimental to the public interest or welfare.

Modern criminal law is derived from the English common law, which recognized three types of crimes: felonies, misdemeanors, and treason, the latter not to be discussed here. Statutes have added new crimes and concepts to the basic common law felonies of murder, manslaughter, rape, sodomy, robbery, larceny, arson, and burglary. Generally felonies are crimes for which the punishment is death or imprisonment in the state prison for more than one year, with other penalties possibly being invoked, such as loss of civil and political rights, professional licenses, and so on. All crimes not felonies are termed misdemeanors.

Certain elements are necessary in order to constitute a crime. One generally says there must be the criminal intent and the criminal act or omission. Mere intent is not punished, but an attempt to commit a crime may be. Intent is provided by circumstantial or direct evidence, but it is usually inferred from the circumstantial evidence. Intent is a frame of mind that leads one to criminal conduct.

Motive differs from intent, for it is the emotional impulse which induces the act, such as hate, greed, envy, fear. Motive does not need to be shown or proven by the prosecution, but it is considered in establishing the presumption of innocence of the accused.

It is necessary to point out that certain criminal offenses do not require showing criminal intent, such as sales of misbranded or impure articles, violations of traffic regulations, and general police regulations for health, safety and welfare.

Criminal negligence may also make an act a crime without criminal intent, such as negligent homicide, so negligence is often an element of crime.

There must also be a criminal act or omission. The act cannot be independent of the intent. Failure to act may be punished where the person is under a duty to act, such as failing to file a tax return or an accident report.

Also required is what is known as the "corpus delicit," a legal concept which does not necessarily mean the murder victim. This concept is extended to refer to the body or elements of the crime, which consist of the fact of the injury or harm done, and the existence of a criminal cause resulting in that injury. This must be proven, not by out of court admissions or confession of the defendant, but by satisfactory evidence apart from this. It may be by circumstantial evidence.

The law considers it a sufficient criminal act where a person attempts to commit a crime but does not succeed. To constitute an attempt there must be the specific intent to commit a certain crime and a direct but unsuccessful act done toward its commission. The act must be such that the crime would have been accomplished were it not for an interruption. In attempting the crime, a person may complete another one, such as murder during an attempted burglary, in which case he will be punished for the crime committed.

It is also considered a criminal act when a person solicits another to commit a specific crime, even though the person may not do so. Urging or inciting is a sufficient criminal act, even if the second party does not do the act.

In some states soliciting a person to commit even a misdemeanor is considered a crime.

A conspiracy is an agreement between two or more persons to do an unlawful act, or to accomplish a lawful act through unlawful means. One or more of the parties is to do the overt act. Thus, a conspiracy is a criminal partnership. The mere unlawful agreement is enough to constitute the crime, however, without commission of the act. Usually in criminal law an unlawful intent is not of itself punished unless it is followed by an act which constitutes the crime or an attempt. It is reasoned that punishing conspiracy as a felony is wise because criminal activities of people acting together are so much more dangerous and more likely to succeed than the intent of an individual acting alone. Each member of a conspiracy is liable for the acts of any of them in carrying out the general aim of the conspiracy—all acts, in other words, that are the reasonable and probable consequences of the common unlawful conspiracy.

Often when a crime is committed, more than one person is involved. The law does not treat equally the various parties to a crime, except in the case of misdemeanors. At common law there are principals in the first degree, who actually commit the crime, and principals in the second degree, for example those present and aiding and abetting in the commission of the crime. The phrase "aid and abet" is often misunderstood. Usually to be liable as an abetter the defendant must have instigated or advised the crime or have been present when it was committed in order to assist. To be guilty he must have taken part in its planning and have taken affirmative action in its commission.

There is usually no difference in the punishment given first and second degree principals. If the crime is the result of two or more required acts, all guilty parties who perform any of these acts are joint principals in the first degree. An illustration of this is where some members of a counterfeiting gang may obtain the paper and ink, another may engrave the plates, and others may pass the money. One does not need to be present at all of these times in order to be a principal.

A principal in the second degree is one who did not do the criminal act himself or with the aid of an innocent agent (like a nurse who unknowingly administers poison to a patient), but is guilty of the felony because of having assisted, advised, ordered or encouraged the crime, whether he was actually or constructively present at the time. If he is absent at the time of commission, he is an accessory before the fact instead. Or he may be what is called constructively present, such as being a lookout at a bank robbery. In other words, he is cooperating with the criminals who are committing the crime, in a position to help them if necessary and to aid in the success of the crime.

Accessories may be accessories before the fact or accessories after the fact, the first being those who may advise about commission of the crime, procure someone to help commit it, and the latter those who after the crime may hide a principal or assist him in escaping. Some states have abolished the differences in punishment as to the parties to the crime, and punish all principals equally with accessories before the fact, except for the one who is the prosecution witness. Since the accessory before the fact is not present physically when the crime is committed, he cannot give aid at that moment, but may have assisted a long time ago. He may simply suggest victims or make general plans for crimes. An accessory after the fact, knowing of the criminal's guilt, gives aid in an effort to prevent his discovery, arrest, trial, or punishment. The aid given must be of a type that tends to frustrate the

4

course of justice. Unlike the accessory before the fact, the accessory after the fact may be present when the crime is committed.

Chapter 2

OFFENSES OR CRIMES AGAINST THE PERSON

HOMICIDE

Homicide is the killing by one human being of another human being. Not every killing is a crime. Common and statutory law usually distinguish between these types of homicide: criminal homicide, murder, manslaughter, second-degree murder, voluntary and involuntary homicide, and justifiable homicide.

The reason for this classification was to divide criminal from non-criminal homicide and to distinguish between the crimes when capital punishment is the penalty and those where it is not. The various states in the United States have made their own distinctions, which will be apparent in the statutory tables in Appendix A.

To constitute homicide, a human being must be killed by another human being. If a man kills an animal, or an animal kills a man, there is no homicide. However, an animal could be the means of doing the killing, such as would be the case if a man loosed a wild animal upon someone. Also, in most states, for the law to recognize homicide, the person must die within a year and a day from the time the act alleged to have caused the death occurred.

The death does not need to have been caused by a positive act, but can be because of an omission or a failure to act where a person is under a legal duty to act, as in a father's failure to provide adequately for his children. But the criminal act must be the proximate cause without intervening causes.

Where there is no intervening factor, the defendant is guilty if death results from his act or omission. If arson results in the death of a person who tries to put out the fire, the arsonist is guilty of murder. Homicide occurring during a robbery is murder. It is not necessary to prove anything but the intent to commit robbery. This common law "felony-murder" rule is sometimes modified if the statutory definition includes the word "purposely" as part of the definition of murder.

If a defendant robs a victim and leaves him lying in the street where he is run over by an automobile, is it murder? This is where an independent force comes in. The rule applied here is that the defendant should reasonably have foreseen that an automobile might have run over his victim. If the intervening cause is foreseeable, the defendant is responsible.

An unborn child at common law could not be the subject of homicide. An injury to a pregnant woman, causing the child to be born dead, was not homicide. For it to be murder or manslaughter the child must be born alive and then later die of the prenatal injuries it received. This is still generally the rule.

MURDER

Murder at common law was defined as the unlawful killing of a human being with malice aforethought. Many of the state laws incorporate this into their definition of murder at the present time. There are two kinds of malice, express and implied. Express is where there is actual intent to kill the person killed. On the other hand, implied malice is where there is an intent to inflict great bodily harm, or where an act is done willfully which has a tendency to cause death or great bodily harm, or where a homicide is committed during the course of some other felony.

Malice is a state of mind where one does not care what consequences developed as far as causing death or great

8

harm. There is a wanton disregard of the probable harm one's conduct may cause, or the actual intent to cause harm. A sniper taking shots at cars on a freeway is acting in this manner.

At common law there were no degrees for murder, and the punishment was death. While our state statutes have modified and changed the common law definition for murder, most of them base it upon the intent to cause the death with deliberation and premeditation. Many of our states have adopted the idea of two degrees of murder, partly in an initial attempt to limit the death penalty. The Commonwealth of Pennsylvania was the first to define the two degrees of murder, and punish only the first with death. The preamble to the Pennsylvania statute indicates that its primary purpose was to limit the death penalty to the most depraved murderers: "The punishment of death ought never to be inflicted where it is not absolutely necessary to the public safety." The most common definition of murder is taken from this Pennsylvania Act of 1794. It defines first degree murder as "all murder which shall be perpetrated by means of poison, or by lying in wait, or by any other kind of willful, deliberate and premeditated killing," and "homicide occurring in the course of the commission or attempt to commit arson, rape, robbery or burglary," the so-called "felony-murder" rule. Approximately one-half of the states follow this definition in varying language. A comparison of the summaries for murder and manslaughter in the appendix will show the different technical definitions used.

The words "deliberation" and "premeditation" as used in these statutes, have also been given technical definitions by the courts. "Deliberation" implies a decision made calmly, with the reasons for and against being examined and weighed, before embarking on a course of action.

9

"Premeditation" implies a previous plan or design for action. In some states the two words are used as synonyms; elsewhere "deliberation" implies reflection, no matter how brief, upon the act before its commission, as distinguished from sudden impulse; while "premeditation" implies a previous design which might include acts on impulse.

Benjamin Cardozo, the famous Supreme Court justice and legal philosopher, felt that one reason behind this describing of the words was a way of allowing a jury "to find the lesser degrees of murder when the suddenness of the intent, the vehemence of the passion seem to call irresistibly for the exercise of mercy."

Another noticeable similarity in the statutes of several states is the inclusion in the definition of first-degree murder of homicides unintentionally committed by an act greatly dangerous to the lives of others, indicating a depraved mind regardless of human life. The courts generally limit the application of this part of the law to cases where the lives of many people have been endangered by some action. Premeditation and deliberation may be inferred from the circumstances surrounding the killing, such as threats made by the defendant in the past, the kind of weapon used, actions after the murder, such as trying to conceal it, etc. Of course the defendant may offer evidence to show his mental state, that he was insane, intoxicated, incapable of premeditating or of malice aforethought. If lying in wait can be shown, no other proof of premeditation is necessary. Here generally the killer must be concealed in ambush.

FELONY-MURDER

In some states the definition of first degree murder includes homicides committed during the perpetration of another felony. This is the felony-murder rule, which is the doctrine that makes it murder to kill a person, innocent bystander or anyone, during the commission of another felony, usually burglary, arson, rape, or robbery. The killing does not need to be intentional, and premeditation and malice are not necessary. The only criminal intent needed is the specific intent to commit a particular felony, the elements of which must be proven. A not unusual example of this is where a rape victim is murdered, or where an innocent bystander is shot by a fleeing robber. The rule has been applied also to cases where one co-conspirator shot another. Certain limits have been placed on this felony-murder rule. For example, in New York the felony must be independent of the homicide or it cannot be a basis for conviction. In California the only requirement is that there must be specific intent to commit the felony, such as burglary, mayhem, robbery. As long as the felony and the murder are parts of a continuous transaction, and the elements of the felony are proven, the felony-murder rule will be followed in that state.

Some state statutes have gone beyond the common law rule by declaring that the commission of any involuntary killing during the course of any unlawful act tending to destroy life is murder. Under Georgia law it was murder for a motorist to kill a pedestrian when he was driving while intoxicated at an excessive speed on the wrong side of the road.

Other states have restricted the felony-murder rule where they do not consider the statutory felony sufficiently dangerous for the application of the rule. In Michigan, where the sale of liquor was a statutory felony, a seller was found not guilty of the death of a customer who died of alcoholism and exposure to the cold. In Pennsylvania it was held that it was not first degree murder where death resulted from the felony of statutory rape.

SECOND DEGREE MURDER

Most states having degrees of murder define second degree murder as all other kinds of homicide which would have been murder at common law. Some define it as murder committed purposely and maliciously but without deliberation and premeditation. In other states homicides evincing a "depraved and malignant heart," as one example, are designated as second degree murder. As was said before, the primary purpose for dividing murder into degrees was to limit the severest punishment to the most serious offenses. The death penalty is not imposed for murder in the second degree.

At times an unlawful killing is found to be second degree murder at the end of a trial because neither side proved it to be something else. The prosecution may prove the elements (corpus delicti) of homicide, but is not able to prove premeditation or sufficient provocation and heat of passion. With this evidence, malice afore-thought is legally presumed, and the pi oper verdict is second degree murder.

MANSLAUGHTER

The crimes of murder and manslaughter constitute just one offense under the early common law of England. Before the laws on the subject, any killing was punishable by death and forfeit of land and other property, but the crime was within benefit of clergy where the life of the criminal could be saved if he qualified. Then the more serious type of homicide, murder with malice afore-thought, was removed from benefit of clergy, the word "murder" was applied to homicide with malice afore-thought, and the term "manslaughter" was invented for the other lesser crime.

Some of the states, as may be seen upon consulting the

Appendix C, have subdivided either or both murder and manslaughter into different degrees. As stated before, murder is distinguished from manslaughter in that it is a homicide that is willful, deliberate or premeditated, committed with malice aforethought, or committed while engaged in perpetrating, or attempting to perpetrate, some other felony. On the other hand, manslaughter will be the crime charged if the provocation is sufficient, such that it would cause a person to act from passion rather than from reason. Insulting words or actions alone are not considered sufficient provocation to reduce a killing from murder to manslaughter, even though some other slight additional act may do so, or may determine the punishment if more than one penalty is allowed by law. The circumstances here are such that the state of mind of the one doing the killing must not be malicious, and he has not actually premeditated the killing as, for example, killing someone in a sudden and angry fist fight, being suddenly and forcefully assaulted, or finding one's wife or husband in an adulterous act. The provocation must be related to the sudden angry passion, and the killing must follow the provocation before the heat of passion cools.

How long a time comprises this cooling-off period depends upon whether, in the time since the provocation was received, the mind of the ordinary reasonable man would have cooled and calmed sufficiently that he would again be acting by reason, not emotion. The test is whether, considering all the circumstances, the provocation and the condition of the accused, a reasonable man under like circumstances would calm himself in that period of time between the provocative act and the killing, or whether, after a lapse of time, he could again become so emotionally stirred and provoked, that he would relive the provactive act and be aroused to sufficient passion to kill without reason or reflection.

13

A person may kill after a long time during which he has been continually provoked, but has controlled his temper time after time, until the final emotional outburst. Passion may also be revived by being brought again to the person's mind after a cooling period, so that he is controlled by that feeling, as where one is confronted by his mother's murderer, and may become provoked enough to lose control and kill.

Some state statutes have divided manslaughter into voluntary, discussed above, which in intentional homicide, and involuntary, unintentional, excusable or negligent homicide, or manslaughter first and second degree. A comparison of the state laws regarding manslaughter reveals that a number distinguish between voluntary and involuntary manslaughter in practically the same terms as the common law. The maximum penalty for voluntary manslaughter is more severe than that for involuntary manslaughter. Some states have followed the New York Penal Code in defining first degree manslaughter as acting with intent to cause serious physical injury and causing death instead, or intending to cause death but doing it under circumstances which do not constitute murder first degree because done under influence of extreme emotional disturbance. Usually then second degree manslaughter is defined as homicide caused by one acting in such a manner as to recklessly cause death, but without the intent to do so. Some states define manslaughter simply as unlawfully killing a person, sometimes adding the words "without malice" and "without deliberation," and provide only one penalty. A number of states do not define the crime, but give the penalty. It is interesting to note that sometimes there is a provision for payment of a heavy monetary penalty in addition to, or instead of, a prison sentence, particularly for second degree manslaughter.

NEGLIGENT HOMICIDE

Just as the line between murder and manslaughter is a shadowy one, so is the line between manslaughter and non-criminal or civil negligence. A homicide resulting from an act unduly dangerous to life or limb may be manslaughter, murder, or civil negligence. Usually the difference between the negligence which is deemed civil wrong and that which is criminal is based on words such as wanton, reckless, gross, culpable, as distinguished from simple or ordinary negligence. The degree of the risk is usually the difference between civil and criminal negligence.

Negligent action causing death is action which falls below the usual standard of care observed by the ordinary prudent man and established by law to protect lives from unreasonable risk of danger. Whoever causes harm as a result of negligence incurs liability. If it is simple negligence, the one harmed would have the right to receive damages; if criminal negligence, the actor is guilty of a criminal offense when his standard of care does not measure up to that of a responsible person. Criminal negligence is usually characterized by reckless conduct. If the act causing death is merely forbidden by law and not otherwise wrong, the death resulting is excusable if not willful or the result of criminal negligence. However, a death resulting from intentional violation of a law resulting from the desire to protect human life, such as an anti-riot law, would be criminal negligence.

JUSTIFIABLE AND EXCUSABLE HOMICIDE

Justifiable and excusable homicides are sometimes termed innocent homicide, in that they do not involve criminal guilt and no blame is attached. Situations arise in everyday life that come within the category of innocent

15

homicide. If commanded by law the homicide is justifiable and therefore not punishable. One example is killing an enemy in battle in wartime, and another is executing a death sentence upon a convicted criminal, one who has committed a capital offense. Homicides authorized by law also include the killing of a criminal in self-defense when the one doing the killing is in imminent danger of death or great bodily harm, and is not himself at fault, the killing of a murderer if necessary in arresting him or in preventing his escape, or killing him if there is great resistance, when a criminal is engaged on committing a felony with great force, such as rape or robbery.

Not all felonies are such as would justify assault or homicide in order to prevent them. A felony that is not accompanied by violence or surprise does not require homicide or force to prevent it. For example, the prevention of the crime of larceny would not justify a homicide. Nor would homicide be justified if done to prevent simple assault and battery, which does not endanger life or threaten great bodily harm.

Homicide which is not commanded or authorized by law is excusable if it is committed under a situation where no criminal guilt is involved. Where one boxer kills another in a state where boxing is legal, the death would be excusable. In a situation where someone is lawfully shooting at a target and without negligence kills someone, that is also excusable, because accidental.

Homicide occurring while a person is defending himself may be either justifiable or excusable. If it occurs during a fight, and self-defense is claimed, the party who was threatened must in some states show that he had retreated as far as possible before taking his opponent's life. The one committing the homicide must believe that his own life is in imminent danger. However, where a person is assaulted in his own home, there is no requirement that he must first retreat. In every case of self-defense the person who kills must not have provoked the fight nor have been the aggressor. Here the homicide is justifiable.

If a practical joke is played upon a person by someone who is a very convincing actor and seems to be a genuine menace, but has a fake weapon, the person threatened may really feel that his life is in danger and kill to protect it. The homicide is here not justifiable, but is excusable because of the mistake of fact. Or if a person is grievously assaulted and attacked, so that killing his assailant is justifiable, but he mistakenly shoots an innocent bystander instead, the homicide is excusable, since the shot was fired without criminal negligence.

CRIMINAL RESPONSIBILITY

Homicides committed by those who are irresponsible are not punished as criminal homicides, even though they are still considered criminal acts. Among those who are considered irresponsible are children, the drunk, and the insane. Under common law children under the age of seven years were presumed incapable of harboring criminal intent and so were not criminally responsible for their actions. In some states the age has been raised to ten years. From seven to fourteen years the common law presumed children incapable of forming criminal intent, but this presumption could be rebutted by showing that the particular child had sufficient intelligence to distinguish between right and wrong. After a child reached the age of fourteen it was presumed that he could form criminal intent, but this presumption could also be rebutted by the accused.

Usually a man who is insane is not criminally responsible for his acts, because he is considered to be incapable of forming a criminal tent. The courts vary as to the test of insanity, but the usual rule is whether the person is capable of distinguishing between right and wrong. This is called the rule of M'Naghten's case. Daniel M'Naghten killed the secretary to the Prime Minister of England, Robert Peel, thinking he was shooting Peel. He was acquitted of the murder on the ground of insanity because of the jury instruction that the defendant should be convicted if he was in a sound state of mind, or acquitted if he did not have the "use of his understanding so as to know he was doing a wrong and wicked act." This 1843 case may be read in Volume Eight of the English reports on page 718. Because of the fact that the intended victim was Prime Minister, the House of Lords after debate asked certain questions of the judges. Their answers were printed with the report of the case, and for this reason the case took on great importance.

Under this rule it must be proven that the accused was under such a defect of reason from disease of the mind that he did not know the nature or quality of the act he was committing, or if he did know, then he did not know that he was doing wrong. The law in this case had been developing in England for centuries, and was thus set by this ruling. In about half of the states this right-wrong test was made the determining factor of criminal incapacity because of a mental disorder, but in the past fifteen years has been modified.

When a homicide is committed by an insane person who has some sane intervals, then it must be determined whether he was sane or insane at the time of the act. His condition at the time of the act determines whether or not he is responsible, but his behavior before and after is considered to determine his condition at the time of the crime.

In some instances drunknness affects a person's responsibility for a homicide. At common law it was no defense to murder, no matter how excessive, and did not excuse or lessen the offense. Even though the person was temporarily deprived of his reason, he was as responsible as a sober person. Intoxication and insanity are not on the same level as far as responsibility or criminal capacity is concerned, because intoxication is usually voluntarily contracted, whether it is intoxication from alcohol or from drugs. In states where there are different degrees of murder, and an actual intent to kill, or deliberation or premeditation, is necessary for murder first degree, but not for second degree, drunkenness may be shown to establish the absence of intent needed for a verdict of murder first degree. However, it would not be a defense to a charge of murder first degree. Nor would it be a defense to a charge of murder second degree where actual intent and premeditation are not required.

If a person is not voluntarily intoxicated, but is so because of the fraudulent scheme of another, and does not realize what he is drinking, or has been forced to drink, criminal incapacity to form intent is not necessarily established. The only sure fact is that the person's behavior is without blame and so is to be dealt with in the same way as if caused by mental disease or a mental defect. Then the person could be shown to have been in such a state of mind that he was incapable of acting with the deliberation and premeditation necessary by law for murder in the first degree. This is not the same as if a person has formed an intent to commit homicide and then had become drunk to strengthen his nerve.

ASSAULT AND BATTERY

At common law assault and battery were considered misdemeanors, though serious ones could be charged as attempts to commit the intended crime, such as murder, rape, etc. At present in some states there is what is termed aggravated assault, such as assault to do great bodily harm, with intent to rape or rob, for example, or assault with a deadly weapon. In other states there are degrees of assault and battery, depending upon how serious the offense is. The greater the seriousness, the greater the punishment.

An assault is an unlawful attempt to commit a battery upon the person of another. A battery is intentional unlawful use of force upon another person. One can have assault without battery, that is, the unsuccessful attempt. The most usual examples of assault and battery are hitting another with a fist, a stick or stone, knifing, or shooting. Inducing a person to take poison, or throwing lye upon him, or exposing a child or an adult to bad weather, all constitute assault and battery, though no physical force is applied directly to the victim.

For the crime to be assault and battery, there must be more than the mere intent to commit a battery or injury. The element of attempt must be shown, that is, a specific intent to commit, coupled with an act that is close to accomplishment and not merely preparation.

In California and a few other states, the person must have the present ability to commit the crime. A threat with an unloaded gun is no crime. While a threat is not enough, there may be difficulty in distinguishing between a threat and the assault. Getting a weapon ready without attempting to use it, or without the ability to use it at the time, probably would not constitute an assault. If someone says, "If you weren't my brother-in-law, I would beat you within an inch of your life," it would not be an assault as there is no intent, but merely a threat without intent to commit injury.

Sometimes an unlawful act causing an injury, although done unintentionally, will be considered a battery instead of an accident. If the act as a crime, and *malum in se* (wrong in itself), and the injury is the natural result of the act, there may be an assault and battery. For example, aiming and shooting a gun into a crowd and hitting someone is assault and battery, or murder or manslaughter if a person is killed. If the act is *malum prohibitum* (a prohibited wrong), an act which is not inherently evil or immoral, but is forbidden by law, such as driving in excess of the speed limit, the driver will not be guilty of assault and battery if he injures someone, but will be civilly responsible. The case might be assault and battery if the person is guilty of gross negligence, such as driving while drunk on the wrong side of a freeway.

It is important to note in connection with assault and battery that great force is not necessary to constitute the crime. Even a touching, both in tort and criminal law, may be sufficient. A degree of force may be enough without any pain or bruising, as, for example, when a man caresses and fondles a woman without her consent, even though he is not overwhelming her with violence.

AGGRAVATED ASSAULT

In most of the states there are laws dealing with felonious assaults and batteries, or what we might call aggravated assault or assault with intent to murder, rob, rape, or do great bodily harm. These crimes would be punished as felonies. To prove aggravated assault it is necessary to show the specific intent to commit the crime of murder, rape, or whatever it is. Specific intent, not apparent intent, is necessary and is usually proved by circumstantial evidence. There must be more than preparation or a threat of harm at some future time, but pointing a loaded gun is usually an assault. Assault with a deadly weapon is usually punished as aggravated assault.

A deadly weapon is one which is likely to cause death if used in the customary manner. The courts usually take note that loaded guns, axes, hammers, etc., are deadly weapons, but leave it up to the jury to decide whether other weapons are deadly within the circumstances of the case. This would include objects like a glass, a stick or a stone.

An assault with intent to commit a particular felony differs from an attempt. For example, a defendant may commit an attempt to commit murder even though he has not yet come close enough to aim or to threaten the person, but an assault would require him to come closer. An attempt may not include an assault, but an assault clearly includes an attempt.

No injury is necessary for a person to be charged with the crime of assault with a deadly weapon. The person's aim may be diverted, so that the person is not shot, but the assault and the intent are there.

A not infrequent method in injuring, or attempting to injure, a person today is by throwing vitriol, a corrosive acid, or a chemical of some kind with the intent to injure or disfigure the person. This is, of course, a felony requiring a specific intent and also usually a showing that some of the acid, however small the quantity, touched the person, and that the act was done willfully and maliciously.

Assault with intent to rape as a crime requires the intent to have intercourse against the woman's will. If the man abandons his attempt, he is guilty only of simple battery.

MAYHEM

The crime of mayhem, an aggravated battery, is defined as disfiguring or maiming a person by depriving

22

him of a part of his body, such as an eye, a limb, an ear, or making it useless. A specific intent to maim or disfigure is not usually necessary, as malice is inferred.

RAPE

Rape is sexual intercourse with a female not the wife of the perpetrator, accomplished without her consent, by force or against her will. Usually only the slightest penetration is necessary.

If the woman is incapable of consenting because of mental condition, immaturity, or because her resistance is overcome by force or fear of harm or a drugged or intoxicated state, the law presumes that there is no consent. Consent obtained by fraud in a pretend marriage, upon pretext of medical treatment, etc., is not true consent. Likewise if someone impersonates the woman's husband, she does not in actuality consent to an act of adultery.

A husband can be guilty of aiding and abetting a third person of raping his wife, or a woman may likewise be guilty of aiding and abetting the rape of another woman.

Present-day cases do not require resistance to the uttermost, where a woman is intimidated either by express or implied threats of great bodily harm. All of the force necessary to achieve intercourse and resistance to prevent it is required to prove the crime, unless the victim is under the age of consent, when the completed crime would be statutory rape. The term "Statutory rape" is not always found in the statute books, but is generally implied to an act of intercourse with a minor, unless she is defendant's wife. Even though no resistance may be offered, or consent is given in such a case, rape is charged as it is presumed that consent cannot be given because of the extreme youth of the female.

KIDNAPING

At common law, kidnaping was a misdemeanor, but under the laws of the states it has been made a felony. When a person is held for ransom, it is treated as a capital offense.

The Lindbergh law and the federal authorities come into the picture when a kidnaped person is taken from one state to another if held for ransom or reward, and the punishment may be death unless the person is freed unharmed. After a person has been kidnaped and held for seven days there is a presumption that he has been taken across state lines, but this presumption is not conclusive.

Asportation, or carrying the person away, is essential to the crime, but the courts have interpreted the carrying away to include such varied acts as moving a person a few feet, locking bank cashiers in a vault, and jumping into a car and ordering the driver at gunpoint to take the defendant elsewhere.

Secrecy is not always essential to proving the crime, although some states have substituted for the asportation an intent to confine the victim somewhere in secret. Taking a person and keeping him against his will is false imprisonment; to seize him unlawfully and keep him in secret is kidnapping.

Chapter 3

PROPERTY OFFENSES

THEFT AND LARCENY

At common law there were legalistic differences between the crimes of appropriation of another's property: larceny, the taking by trespass—embezzlement, misappropriation of funds by a trustee or fiduciary—and false pretenses, the obtaining of property by false representations. These terms did not serve any useful purpose, and in a number of states, such as California, these crimes were combined in the Penal Code into "theft," whereas in other states, such as New York, all three were combined under the name, "larceny."

The purpose of combining these crimes was to avoid specifying in the indictment charging theft whether the crime is embezzlement, larceny or false pretenses, and thus avoiding the technical difficulties in pleading and proof required by the common law. However, these common law differences still exist in substance even where they have been abolished in form.

Larceny is the taking by trespass and carrying away of any personal property of another of at least nominal value, with intent to steal it. At English common law it was one of the few felonies, but under the laws of the United States it may be either a felony or a misdemeanor depending upon the value of the property that has been stolen. Under common law the thing taken had to be personal property, but statutory law has extended this to include severing and carrying away things in the nature of real property, trees, crops, etc., which are capable of being carried away.

The things taken must be capable of ownership. Taking an abandoned property or treasure trove cannot be larceny, for the real owner has given up possession and title. Wild animals are not property. Water, oil, gas and electricity are considered property after they have been confined in pipes, reservoirs, etc., and reduced to possession in some way. If they can be appropriated by someone not their owner, they can be the subject of larceny.

Under the law of larceny we consider who has possession of the article, not the title; a person may be the rightful possessor, such as a bailee, without having title. The one holding title may be guilty of larceny if he removes an automobile from a garage without paying a repair bill thereon. Also, it can be larceny to steal an article from the possession of a thief although the article was acquired and reduced to possession illegally. Here one must distinguish between possession, custody and title. A person shopping in a store may be guilty of larceny if he takes from the store, without intending to pay for it, an object turned over to him for examination, because he has custody only. However, he may have the same article delivered to his home by the store without intending to pay for it and not be guilty of larceny because the delivery to his home transferred possession to him. The driver of the delivery truck has custody of the article only. If the person pays for the goods by worthless check, it could also be larceny.

It is not larceny to take one's property from someone who has no right to hold it. If you sell furniture to someone who takes it and some other articles from your home, it is not larceny to take back the things not sold to him while he is loading them on his truck.

The taking of possession of an article is not sufficient for larceny unless the taking is by trespass, that is, without the consent of the owner. If the consent has not been obtained through trickery or force, there is no larceny, however. Leaving on article carelessly lying somewhere does not mean that consent to taking it is given. This is a technical trespass, and does not refer to trespass on real estate.

The manner of the taking is irrelevant. The property may be carried away by the actual theif in his hands, or it may be taken by tapping an electric conduit and consuming it without passing it through a meter. Or the property may be taken by an innocent person, as a young child or an insane person, who does not know the facts. Or a person may have an innocent go between deliver property to him, as when he steals a trunk by changing baggage checks at a railroad station and having the case wrongfully delivered to him. But if the property is taken from the owner through violence or by putting him in fear of trouble, the offense is not larceny but robbery.

Taking "sufficient for larceny" means that at some moment the thief must have complete independent and absolute possession and control of the thing taken. If he merely puts his hand on a woman's purse in a shopping cart but does not take it into his hand, it would not be larceny. Or if he touches a pen attached to a chain in a library, but does not break the chain, it is not larceny. The possession may be merely momentary, and the length of time the taker holds the article does not matter, if there is a sufficient carrying away of the article to meet the requirement of the crime. If the article has been segregated or moved slightly from its original position, but not from the premises, it may be a sufficient carrying away, such as where goods are concealed under a person's clothing, but he is apprehended before he can leave the building.

Larceny of an animal can be accomplished by bringing it under the thief's control and only slightly carrying it away, placing it in a pen or container. Chasing it without catching it would not be larceny. Killing cattle is not larceny unless the defendant takes possession of the hide or body and carries it away, unless the taking away has been eliminated by the statute of the particular state where the crime was committed. Altering or removing a brand from cattle with an intent to steal them might be considered larceny even in a state which had a requirement of carrying away as an element of the crime.

The time of day or night is not a material element in deciding whether or not the crime has been committed, although it may affect the seriousness of the offense if the statute divides larceny into degrees and makes it a more serious offense when occurring at nighttime. The place is also immaterial; it may be a store, dwelling, car, warehouse, or the person of the owner. Taking from the person of the owner makes it a more serious offense in some states.

An essential element of the crime of larceny is wrongful intent, intent to steal or some knowledge that the act is wrongful. Borrowing or taking by mistake is not larceny, nor is it where one acts on good faith that he has permission from the true owner. If the article is taken with an intent to buy, or under good faith claim or right, it is not larceny, even though the claim may be based upon a misconception of law. An example of this is a taking by a creditor of property to satisfy his debt, where he is honestly mistaken that he has the right to be paid.

Another essential element is appropriation or deprivation of the owner. There must be intent to deprive the owner permanently of his property and an intent to appropriate it to the taker's use or to a use inconsistent with the right of the person from whom the article is taken. If there is no statute to the contrary, it is not larceny to borrow an automobile or bicycle without permission, since the taker does not intend to deprive the owner permanently of his possession.

The crime of "joy-riding" deserves special mention. It

was more prevalent before automobiles were so numerous, perhaps, and there was great temptation on the part of young boys in particular to drive a car without the consent of the owner. Since these automobiles were taken with the intent to use them for a short time only, and then return them to the owners, the crime of larceny could not be charged without special statutes. Therefore the laws provided a penalty for this taking without intent to steal, making it a felony because of the damage that often resulted to the car, its high cost, and also because in larceny of motor vehicles it was difficult to secure a conviction because the thief could claim he did not intend to keep the car.

A more or less common occurrence is when the intent to appropriate to the taker's use occurs after the taking, if the original taking was without the consent of the owner or through fraud. If the defendant cannot form an intent at the time of taking because he is intoxicated, but forms the intent to convert the property to his own use when he becomes sober, then he has committed larceny. If a person is overpaid innocently, and after discovering the error uses the money for himself, he would not be guilty of larceny, but if he receives the overpayment knowingly with an intent at that time to use the excess, he would be guilty of larceny. His possession may be lawful if he acquires the goods by fraud or deceit, but if he does so with an intent to steal, it would be larceny. If he receives the goods for a particular purpose but then converts it so some other use, it is larceny if at the time he receives the article he has the intent to appropriate if for himself.

Generally, if the owner delivers property intending to give possession and title, the person taking it would not be guilty of larceny in receiving it, even though he induced delivery through fraud. He would then be guilty of the crime of false pretenses, discussed below. However, in some states this is still larceny if the title does not pass until certain conditions are met.

DEGREES OF LARCENY

The Statute of Westminister in England in 1275 classified larceny as either grand or petit (now petty), the former being a felony and a capital offense, the latter punishable by loss of goods and whipping. The classification depended upon the value of the goods stolen. Modern statutes usually retain this classification, and the amount varies between $50 and $200 as the dividing line between the two types of larceny, with the theft of some specifically named articles being automatically grand larceny. In California, for example, for a grand theft charge personal property must be of the value of $200; citrus fruits, avocadoes, olives, nuts, and artichokes of the value of $50.

The object stolen must have some legally recognized value. In California, where a lottery was illegal, a winning lottery ticket was not considered a thing of value. If there is no provision in the law for determining value, the rule is the market value of the thing stolen at that time and place. If there is no market value, it is the worth considering all the facts and circumstances in evidence. State statutes usually provide in the case of a stolen note that the value is the amount of money due and collectible on it, or in the case of books or bonds the market value, not the face value. The value of electricity or gas stolen from the owner is the price at which it is sold to the public. If property owned by the federal government is stolen, the crime is a felony if the value is over $100, or a misdemeanor if the value is less. This law also states that value is par, face, market value, or cost price, wholesale or retail, whichever is the greater sum.

Some states provide more severe penalties for larceny from dwelling houses, or from certain other places such as railcars, boats, and trailers.

FALSE PRETENSES

The crime of false pretenses actually means the crime of obtaining property by false pretenses, and was created by statute to fill a gap in the law of larceny, to which it is closely related. This occurred first in England in the time of the colonization of the New World, so was generally accepted in our common law. The new law was necessary because one requirement of the crime of larceny is that the property must be taken without the consent of the owner, and so did not cover cases where the owner was passing title to the property as well as possession, when induced to do so by fraud or deception.

Our states have enacted special statutes and have gone beyond the original law, making it a crime to obtain money, intangible personal property, deeds to real property, executing a check with knowledge that the drawer has insufficient funds, etc. In California the law even includes labor or services where employees are hired without their being advised of labor claims and judgments the employer has been unable to meet.

The elements of the crime of false pretenses are that there must be an intent to defraud, misrepresentation of a present or past fact, and actual reliance by the owner on the defendant's representation. In addition there must be an actual defrauding or the obtaining of something of value without compensation, before the person can be charged with the crime.

Intent to cheat is usually regarded as essential, but it is the intent to defraud, not the intent to receive benefit or advantage from the cheat, that is important. For example, in Texas the law specifically states that where there is a willful intent to receive a benefit or cause an injury, it is of no account that the benefit or injury does not result.

The false representation must be of a past or present fact, not something to take place in the future, and may be implied from the conduct of the defendant, such as hiding something or not disclosing it when there is a duty to speak, or it may be made expressly. A promise without a representation of an existing fact is not sufficient in the absence of a law making it so. Mere "puffing," the usual salesman's talk, is not misrepresentation, upon the theory that a certain amount of it is customary and expected. Predictions of future profits are not a misrepresentation. False promises are made by false pretenses by law, and the prosecution must show the fraudulent intent, not merely that the promises have not been fulfilled. Opinions, if they are understood to be only opinions, are not false pretenses.

Examples of false representations that are frequently made are as to ownership of property, the kind or quality or condition of property, the assets of business, credit, financial position, bills that have been paid, fake cancer cures, and the like.

The test the court uses in determining what the crime is is not whether the false pretenses would deceive an ordinary reasonable man, but whether or not the particular man who gave up his money or property was deceived. In this way the law protects those with little business sense, the gullible and the foolish.

The owner of the property must turn it over in reliance upon the false pretenses, or there is no crime. If the owner has made independent investigation as to the deal, and acts upon his findings, there is likewise no crime any more than there would be if the owner knows or believes the pretense to be false. If the pretense is made later, after the property is obtained, then the crime has not been committed either. In other words, there must be a connection between the transfer of the property and the false representation. The representation may be looked upon as continuing, where there is a time between the representation and the transfer, but the representation must be before.

The pretense may be oral or written, by act or word. Some states require that it be written. In some states where a fact is not disclosed by someone bound to reveal it, that is considered a false pretense. Thus, silence may be the false representation when one is under a duty to speak.

It is interesting to note that the defendant cannot usually bring up the defense that he has given something of value in exchange for the other property. If a person is defrauded he did not get what he contracted for, even though he may not have suffered a net financial loss. If he recovers the property, he has still been the victim of the crime.

Giving a worthless check with the knowledge that there are insufficient funds to cover the check is generally considered a false pretense, but some of the states have special statutes to cover this "cheating by check." The theory on which this is based is that the drawer of the check obtains money by means of the check, and represents by writing it that he has funds in the bank sufficient to cover it. But the person who has given something of value for the check has the right to believe that there are funds in the bank, so that he will be paid. If the drawer discloses that he does not have the funds to cover the check, it relieves him of any guilt in the matter, and it is treated in many states as an extension of credit to the drawer. If a check is post-dated, and the drawer has asked not to have it cashed immediately, the check statutes are not violated.

EMBEZZLEMENT

At common law there was no crime of embezzlement. This too was created by statute, and was designed to cover the crime of misappropriation of property by someone to whom it had been entrusted in good faith. The various states define the crime variously, but it generally consists of fraudulent conversion, appropriation or withholding of the property of another by the one to whom it was lawfully entrusted. The embezzler usually is someone with whom there has been a relationship of trust or confidence.

In the crime of embezzlement one usually thinks of money or securities that have been unlawfully misappropriated, but personal and real property may also be taken in this manner, for example, traveler's checks executed in blank, leased personal property, or a deed to land.

The original taking must be lawful and with the consent of the owner, so the crime differs in this way from theft or larceny. Very often, however, the crime of embezzlement is included in the definition of theft, and is punished as grand or petty theft according to the value of the property taken.

The owner must have at least a recognizable legal interest, if not title, in that property. The relationship between him and the defendant must be one of trust and confidence, so the latter may be agent, employee, lessee, servant, conditional buyer, guardian, executor, bailee, as each state enumerates in its law. In the case of employees or agents, there is no difference between permanent or temporary ones.

The appropriation of the property must be done with fraudulent intent to use it in a manner the owner does not consent to. A person acting in good faith is not guilty of embezzlement, and if accused, he has a right to show that his intent is not fraudulent. Also, a person cannot embezzle his own property, so if he can show a claim of title, he is innocent.

Refusing to pay a debt is not embezzlement, nor is borrowing and keeping an object for too long a time. In the latter case if there is no direct or circumstantial evidence to show that the person has stopped being a borrower, he has not become an embezzler automatically. In some states the person must give up the article upon demand, or account for it in some way. Offering to restore embezzled money or property before being brought to court for the crime usually is considered a mitigating circumstance by the court, although in the case of larceny it does not help the defendant.

FORGERY

Forgery was a misdemeanor at common law, but it is usually a felony in our state statutes. It consists of making a false written instrument with intent to defraud, altering a genuine instrument in a material way, or uttering a forged instrument. In this sense the word "utter" means to offer or pass for value received. The "instrument" is a writing which, if genuine, would be a bill, note, or other paper which would create a legal right or obligation.

There are many ways in which the false instrument may be made. It may be printed, typed, engraved, written with pen or pencil, or it may have been genuine and then altered by erasing part, filling in a name or order words in a blank, signing another's name without authority, and the like.

There must be a writing, such as a fictitious or falsely altered check, bill, note for payment of money by a person or organization, perhaps nonexistent, and there must also be an intent to defraud. Using a genuine instrument for the purpose of defrauding another is not forgery. While it is forgery to sign another's name on a note without authority, with intent to defraud, because this makes the note seem to be the note of the person whose name as agent, falsely claiming that he has authority to bind his so-called principal. The person in that case is guilty of false pretenses, for the instrument is not a false representation, but just what it appears to be on its face. Also, to defraud another person, the instrument must appear to be true in order to defraud a person or put him at a disadvantage. If it is clearly void or illegal on its face, it is not a forgery.

While the intent to defraud is a requirement, it is not necessary that the defrauding is actually accomplished. The test is not whether anyone has been defrauded, but whether anyone might have been, unless the law of the particular state requires proof of actual injury. The intent may be inferred from circumstantial evidence, such as unauthorized signing, false explanations, or taking proceeds of the note or whatever it is for personal use.

As was stated above, "uttering" the forged instrument is passing it to another, knowing it is false. It is not necessary that the one passing it be the forger himself, if he knows of the forgery and intends to defraud by using it. The forger himself may be convicted of both forgery and uttering or of either crime, but is usually punished for only one offense where one instrument is involved. An offer as well as actual passing constitutes the crime of uttering. The maker of the false instrument himself may be guilty of uttering if he has someone else do it; he then is aiding and abetting. Several states punish the one who merely has possession of a false instrument with knowledge of its falsity with an unlawful purpose in mind. As in other crimes, one may also be punished for attempting to utter.

COUNTERFEITING

Counterfeiting is usually thought of as unlawfully making false money in imitation of genuine coinage or paper money. The crime may also extend to other kinds of imitation, and generally covers postage stamps, notes, bankpapers, tickets, certificates, counterfeiting equipment like dies and plates, and bonds.

Since issuance of coinage, stamps, etc., is the prerogative of the federal government, it is usually thought of as a federal crime, but it is also punishable under state statutes, as prosecution is not reserved to the federal courts.

Since a counterfeit is made as an imitation of the genuine article, the resemblance must be such as to deceive a person who is using ordinary caution. If there is no resemblance to a real coin, the article cannot be considered counterfeit money, for example.

Since the advent of so many vending machines requiring the use of coins, there are special statutes providing penalties for manufacturing or selling tokens or slugs which could be used to operate these machines. If a slug is used to obtain a product from a vending machine, the person doing so could be convicted of common-law larceny.

Changing color of stamps, forging overprints, using parts of cancelled stamps to produce one apparently usused stamp, are all considered counterfeiting.

Intent to defraud is not required in counterfeiting of coins, for the purpose for which the coins are made is not important. The only required intent is the intent to make the coin or stamp. But intent to defraud is required in making and passing of paper money, false obligations of securities of the government, and at times for possession of the same.

RECEIVING STOLEN PROPERTY

Receiving stolen goods, knowing them to have been stolen, was a crime at common law, and has not been changed substantially by the statutes. The crime is usually a felony, and is typically thought of as purchase of "hot" jewelry or other objects by a "fence," who conceals the goods from the police until he can sell them to another at a large profit.

The elements of the crime are that the property must have been stolen from someone, it must have been bought or receiving and concealed by the defendant, who must have known that it was stolen and received it for a fraudulent or unlawful purpose.

The receiver must have the property under his control, but not necessarily in his actual possession. Constructive control is all that is needed, if possession is taken by his servant or agent under his direction. The crime does not concern itself much with the thief but rather with the receiver, as the essential is that of receiving the property with the knowledge that it is stolen. The thief's identity may be unknown and is immaterial. Anyone who conceals or withholds property after learning that it is stolen is also guilty of the crime, where the statute includes the concealing of stolen property. The thief himself cannot be considered the receiver.

To convict a person of the crime it is necessary to show that the property was stolen, and that it was stolen property at the time the accused received it. He does not need to know when it was stolen or from whom. The receiver must also have a fraudulent intent in accepting the property. If he takes it with the idea of returning it to the true owner, he would not be guilty of receiving stolen property, as if he had received it for the purpose of helping the thief.

ROBBERY

Robbery, another common-law felony, is in reality a combination of larceny and assault. It may be defined as the felonious taking and carrying away of the personal property of another from his person or in his presence, against his will and by violence, or by putting him in fear. All of the elements of the crime of larceny must be present: the thing taken must be the subject of larceny and personal property belonging to another, there must be taking and carrying away, which must be with wrongful intent to deprive the owner of his property permanently. The added circumstances that make the crime robbery instead of larceny are that the property must be removed from the person of another, or in his presence or control, without his consent but also by violence or causing him to fear. Giving back the thing taken does not constitute a defense to the crime. In jurisdictions which have different degrees of the crime of robbery, first degree would involve violence or fear because of the fact that the criminal is armed with a deadly or dangerous weapon or has been torturing the victim.

If the gun looks real, but is only a toy, the offense is not mitigated by the fact that it really is a toy if it fooled the victim. If the weapon can be used as a club, it is still dangerous if not deadly. If it is not loaded, and the victim does not know this, it is dangerous, for brandishing it about in a threatening manner can cause the victim to be in fear. If the robber does not have a gun at first, but takes the victim's gun away from him, he is still guilty o robbery.

The requirement of taking in the presence of the victim is usually satisfied by a taking from his constructiv presence, from another room of his home, from a plac where he could hear the robbers. As in the crime o larceny, the taking away need not be for a great distanc or out of the presence of the victim.

There must be some slight violence at least, or puttin the victim in fear. Taking the property by a trick, or b picking the victim's pocket, does not constitute violenc If the owner resists the attempt to take his property, eve to a very slight degree, and his resistance is overcom there is considered to be sufficient violence. The strugg or resistance must be during or before the taking, n after.

The requirement of fear does not mean great terro but simply fear of injury to the victim or his family, s that he gives in to the unlawful demand for his propert under reasonable apprehension of danger. Reasonab fear of death or great bodily harm is sufficient to mal the taking of property robbery. Even fear of injury property may be sufficient, such as giving in because of threat to burn down one's home. Fear of injury to on character or reputation is not sufficient to make t taking of property robbery.

Chapter 4

HABITATION OFFENSES

BURGLARY

Burglary is an offense against the security of the habitation ("a man's home is his castle" idea), rather than an offense against property. The purpose of this is to protect the individual in the peaceful occupancy of his home, be it cottage or mansion. At common law burglary is the breaking and entering of the dwelling house of another at night with the intent to commit a felony therein. This definition has been incorporated into criminal statutes of many states, but through the years it has been greatly modified, as a study of the charts in the appendix will show.

The word "breaking" does not necessarily mean damaging the property in any way. It is simple the opening of a door or window, one which does not even need to be locked. Coming in through an open door is not breaking, but if the defendant comes through an open front door and then opens a door that leads from a hallway to a bedroom, for example, he may be guilty of breaking and entering. If, however, he merely breaks open a box or trunk and not a part of the house, it would not be burglary. One may commit breaking and entering by coming down a chimney.

There are some instances where not breaking in the real sense as defined above takes place, but the law regards the entering as constructive entry. This may be where a person enters a house by trick or fraud, with felonious intent. Another example is where someone would pose as a policeman, or has the occupant open the door by some pretense, and he enters to commit a felony. If violence is threatened, or the owner or occupant opens the door because of fear of violence, and the defendant enters with felonious intent, there is also constructive breaking and he would be guilty of burglary. If a servant or employee in a conspiracy opens the door and lets in the defendant for the purpose of committing a felony, both would be guilty of burglary.

Entry is one of the requirements for burglary as well as breaking. If no entry is made, it is not burglary to break open a door or window with intent to enter and commit a felony. This is attempted burglary. The merest entry, however, is sufficient if the felonious intent is there. It may be only a part of the body, such as a hand inserted through an open window to turn a key on a nearby door. It may even be some implement or tool, such as a hook for the purpose of stealing something.

One cannot commit burglary by breaking and entering a house or room he has a right to enter, such as a room or apartment shared with someone else, even if the person has the intent to steal his roommate's property.

At common law there was the requirement that both breaking and entering must be at nighttime, although not necessarily on the same night. In many states breaking and entering in the daytime is also punishable as burglarly under the statutes, but is usually a less serious offense. Statutory changes have also added to the type of buildings where breaking and entering with felonies intent constitutes burglary. In addition to dwelling place in the strictest sense, all other sorts of habitations are included: motels, boats, mobile homes, as well as buildings like factories, schools, railroad cars, and the like.

Many courts consider that where a person enters a house without breaking and then breaks out in order to escape, it is not burglary at common law. The reason is that this is not breaking with a felonious intent, for the intent is to get away. In some of the states, however, by statute this is sufficient to constitute burglary. The laws which require breaking but not entering will cover the cases of breaking out as well as breaking in.

At common law it was not necessary for anyone to be in the house at the time of the breaking and entering, but by statute in some states the absence of a person within makes the offense less serious, such as in New York State, where there are different degrees of burglary. The house or dwelling broken into must be the house of a person other than the accused, but it may be simply another room in the same rooming house or another apartment in the building where the accused lives. A home used for only a part of a year, such as a summer cottage, may also be burglarized. The test is not ownership but lawful occupancy. The real owner of a house can commit burglary if he breaks and enters, with intent to commit a felony, a house belonging to him which he has rented to a tenant.

The intent to commit the felony may be proven by inference from the circumstances surrounding the case. If the felony was actually committed, it can be clearly inferred that the intent to commit the felony existed when the breaking and entering occurred. Even if no felony is committed, the intent may be inferred from the actions of the defendant. For example, if he breaks and enters a house at night, where there are valuable objects, and there is not other motive apparent, it may be inferred that the accused had the intent to steal, and he can be found guilty of burglary. It is not necessary that the felony be committed, for the intent is sufficient for the crime of burglary with the breaking and entering. If the felony is indeed committed, the accused may be found guilty of both the burglary and the particular felony.

In situations where not all of the elements of the crime of burglary are proven, the person may still be found guilty of other crimes, such as criminal trespass, larceny, attempted burglary, possession of burglar's tools, and attempted breaking and entering.

ARSON

Arson at common law was a felony, the malicious burning of the house of another by day or night. Punishment, appropriately enough, was death by burning at one time. Modern statutes have sometimes added the word willful, although it does not seem to mean more than malicious, nor add to the meaning, just as the words "day or night" do not actually add anything. However, under some statutes the punishment is not so severe when arson occurs in the daytime, undoubtedly because most people are awake at that time and can escape more easily.

If a person burns his own building arson is not committed in some states, but if the fire spreads and other buildings burn, he does commit unintentional arson. Here he is not acting maliciously or with ill will, but may have burned it to collect insurance. In many states burning with intent to defraud the insurer is a separate part of the arson statute, with a penalty not as serious as that for first degree arson.

Statutes in our states have also broadened the scope of the crime of arson in extending it to include buildings other than dwelling houses, such as shops, factories, unoccupied houses, one's own property, other real or personal property.

Actual burning of some part of the house or other building is required to constitute the crime. An attempt to burn by setting a fire is not enough, if the house does not burn, but the person may be punished for the attempt. No part of the building needs to be destroyed, so long as there is burning or charring of wood, even though the fire may go out by itself. Mere blackening or discoloration caused by smoke or heat is not arson.

The means used to start the fire is unimportant. It may be by setting fire to rags soaked in gasoline, simply by using matches, by using explosives if the building burns instead of merely blowing up, or by burning an adjoining structure of some kind which spreads the fire.

Where statutes have broadened the common-law definition of arson, the crime is no longer essentially a crime against security of habitation, but against property. Actual burning of some part, however, is still usually an element of the crime. Most states used the words willful or malicious or both, but usually interpret this to mean not negligently nor accidentally. Many have also divided the crime into degrees, providing the worst penalty for dwelling houses, especially when people are therein, or when the burning is at night. Attempted arson is also punishable in many jurisdictions.

Chapter 5

CRIMINAL PROCEDURE

When a person suspected of a crime is apprehended, what happens to him? Although the laws of the various states differ in detail, there are certain basic principles that are common to them all, and a brief outline of criminal procedure may be of interest.

THE ROLE OF THE POLICE

The police play a dual role, for they are effective not only in preventing crime, but in detecting it when committed and in seeing to it that the criminal is arrested so that he may be brought to justice. Through patrolling by car and on foot they can help prevent crime by being in areas where it is most likely to be committed, so that their presence act a deterrent. They respond to the complaints of citizens who are the victims of crime, and then are called upon to use scientific methods of crime detection. Where the police are well-trained, of high caliber, and are sufficient in numbers, the incidence of crime is apt to be lower than in cities where there is insufficient money to keep enough good men on the force.

Within fairly broad limits, the police have considerable discretion as to how and where they will patrol, and what kind of search they will make for criminals, and the methods of detection they will employ and what kinds of programs of crime prevention they will use.

A police officer has authority to arrest a suspect without a warrant when he has reasonable cause to believe that this suspect committed a felony, even though the officer did not see the crime being committed. In a great many states this is also the rule for misdemeanor arrests, although in some the officer must see the

47

misdemeanor committed or have a warrant. Since 1962, when *Wong Sun v. U.S.,* 371 U.S. 471, was decided by the United States Supreme Court, a warrant may be issued only by a judicial officer after he has weighed impartially the information which the police officer believes is probable cause for the arrest. There must be more evidence than suspicion, but not necessarily enough for conviction. A mistake on the part of the police at this early stage may jeopardize the entire case if the arrest is illegal. Arresting a person known by the police to have a record of prior convictions for gambling is not probable cause.

The police may use only the force believed necessary to accomplish the arrest, but an officer is acting at his own peril if he uses a gun. If the crime is a misdemeanor or there is only a suspicion of a felony, use of a gun is not justified.

The police have an implied right to stop suspected people on the street for questioning and frisking, but there is no high court decision on this matter. The circumstances must be such that there is a reasonable ground for investigation, or if there is reason to believe the person to be dangerous, especially if he is searched as well as questioned. A policeman also has the right to ask a person to go with him to the police station. If the person consents, there is no unlawful detention and no arrest. Related to this is the New York "stop and frisk" law, which has also become law in other jurisdictions, and which the United States Supreme Court upheld in opinions by Chief Justice Warren.

BOOKING

When the suspect is brought to a station house, the arresting policeman files a report, and the circumstances are reviewed administratively by the officer on duty or the desk sergeant. Unless the review determines that the person should be released, he is "booked." This consists of noting on the station records a description of the suspect, the reason for his arrest, the time, the charge against him, etc. The suspect is then placed in jail.

BAIL OR DETENTION

If the suspect is accused of a misdemeanor, he may be eligible for release on bail or on "O.R." (his own recognizance), a promise to appear to answer to the charge against him at a later date. In the case of a felony, he cannot be released except after an appearance before a judicial officer. This should be done without unnecessary delay so that the person's constitutional rights under the Fifth Amendment are not violated. It is at this time that the suspect may be questioned by the police, as a part of their investigation of the crime. However, recent decisions of the United States Supreme Court have largely undermined this important means for detection of crime. Confessions obtained during overlong detention of an individual before his arraignment may be illegal; hence they would not be admissible as evidence. In the light of recent cases it seems clear that a person may not be detained for questioning at the expense of his right to speedy arraignment, right to counsel, and right to remain silent until his lawyer or one appointed for him by the court is available.

ROLE OF THE PROSECUTOR OR DISTRICT ATTORNEY

In criminal cases the prosecuting or district attorney is the representative of the municipality or county, or in the case of appeals, of the state. He is usually elected, and serves as the chief administrator of his office, with deputy attorneys and trial attorneys working under him in felony and misdemeanor sections. In some states, such as California, the prosecutor usually plays a very important role in deciding whether or not to continue a prosecution after studying the report of the arresting officer. He may decide, if the person is a first offender, that he should be given another chance; or if mentally ill, that he should be committed; or if the case is weak, that the prosecution should be dropped. In most major felonies, such as murder, the prosecutor's office is on the case right at the beginning, so that he can be in charge of the case and direct operations.

If the decision is to prosecute, the complaint is prepared, giving the name of the defendant and the charge, with a warrant for his arrest. In some states there must first be a meeting of the grand jury, a group of citizens whose duty it is to hear the evidence and bring an indictment to try the case, if a *prima facie* case has been made out, that is, if all of the evidence taken together is such as would justify a conviction if not contradicted or explained at the trial. The indictment, which is probably made out by the district attorney, is voted upon by the grand jury and filed. The defendant is not present at the convening of the grand jury.

Then the defendant's attorney is notified of the date of the arraignment to the indictment. At the arraignment the charge in the indictment is stated to the defendant and he is then asked how he pleads to it. There are several pleas that are possible: guilty, not guilty, guilty of a lesser offense, not guilty by reason of insanity, prior conviction or acquittal of that offense. The question of bail comes up again at this time, at least if the crime is a felony.

If the crime is a misdemeanor and the defendant pleads guilty, he is usually sentenced at once. If he pleads not guilty, he may be tried at once if the arresting officer and complaining witness are both present. In other cases the trial, usually without a jury, will be held in about two or three weeks.

In felony cases, the trial may not come up for several months. Then the first step will be to select the jury which should be done carefully to make sure that it is unbiased and impartial. There are rules and procedure for insuring this. The case then proceeds. First the prosecuting attorney makes an opening statement to the jury, telling the charge, the issues in the case, the evidence that will be offered to prove the case. The counsel for the defendant then makes his opening remarks, asking that the jury keep an open mind until all facts are heard. The prosecuting attorney places his witnesses on the stand first since he has the burden of proof, as it is called, to show that the defendant is guilty beyond a reasonable doubt. The witnesses are cross-examined by the opposing attorney to see if they can give any other facts that might help the defendant, or that might show whether they are lying or biased. After the prosecutor's case is presented, the defense counsel may make several motions to the court, possibly asking that the indictment be dismissed on the ground that the prosecutor has failed to prove guilt beyond a reasonable doubt. If the motions are overruled, he then presents his case for the defense, bringing out testimony and evidence favorable to the defendant, trying to explain the circumstances surrounding the case in such a way that the defendant can be excused, such as proving the self-defense when there is a charge of murder against his defendant.

The prosecutor may bring a rebuttal witness, then makes his summation or closing remarks. Defense counsel will then discuss the evidence, point out inconsistencies in the prosecutor's case, comment on the testimony of

51

witnesses and the impressions they made, and emphasize the facts which the jury should infer from the evidence to support the innocence of his client. The judge then explains the law to the jury, charging them with instructions to guide them in reaching their decision from the facts and evidence presented. When the jury's verdict is presented, the defendant is released if innocent. If found guilty, defendant has several pleas and motions available to him. His counsel may move for a new trial on the ground of error in the trial, on the ground of newly discovered evidence, etc. Another usual move is to appeal to a higher court, which reviews the record and either grants or denies the new appeal. The appeal must be made within a certain time, or it is barred. The defendant is then either set free or returned to jail to await sentencing, usually at a later date.

If the defendant had not been financially able to retain counsel, he would still have been protected under our laws, under which basically he has a constitutional right to have an attorney representing him at every stage of the proceedings in a criminal case. The court may appoint an attorney from among the members of the bar who volunteer to serve without fee. Or there may be a public defender's office or legal aid foundation, the former supported by public funds and the latter perhaps by a combination of public funds and aid from a private charitable foundation.

The defendant may also waive his right to counsel and conduct his own defense, but the court may assign counsel regardless if it considers him incompetent to act as his own attorney.

Thus every effort is made to insure that people accused of crimes are protected against injustice and given their constitutional rights.

Chapter 6

THE DEATH PENALTY-CAPITAL PUNISHMENT

In 1972, a split 5-4 Supreme Court reached a landmark decision, *Furman v. Georgia,* 408 U.S. 428, which held that "imposition and carrying out of the death penalty (constitutes) cruel and unusual punishment in violation of the Eighth and Fourteenth Amendments."

All state and federal law imposing the death penalty must be consistent with provisions of the United States Constitution. In addition, all state laws must be consistent with the constitutions of the state in question. However, litigation over the issue is mainly in terms of the federal constitution, and it is that body of legal principles which is most relevant to our discussion here. The Eighth Amendment provides that no "cruel and unusual punishments may be inflicted". and the courts have often had to determine whether the imposition of the sentence of death is in breach of this provision. Any law which is determined to be in breach of what is laid down in the Constitution is invalid. If, therefore, a death penalty statute is unconstitutional, the death penalty may not be applied.

Legal argument has focused on whether the death penalty is inherently "cruel and unusal" and/or whether it deprives its intended victims of the constitutional guarantees of "due process of law" or the "equal protection of the laws". "Due process of law" may be understood in general terms as "compliance with the fundamental rules for fair and orderly proceedings"; "equal protection of the laws" may be similarly understood as "a guarantee of uniformity of treatment under law of all persons in like circumstances.".

In 1976, *Gregg v. State of Georgia,* 429 U.S. 1301, the Supreme Court held, 7-2, that the punishment of death for *murder* did not invariably constitute "cruel and unusual punishment", and therefore did not in all circumstances violate the United States Constitution. The ruling upheld the death penalty in Florida, Georgia, and Texas, but struck down the laws in North Carolina and Louisiana as being too rigid in requiring capital punishment for certain crimes. The Court ruled that North Carolina's mandatory death sentence of first degree-murder did not meet "objective standards to guide, regularize, and make rationally reviewable the process for imposing the sentence of death. . . . (The) statute provides no standards to guide the jury in its inevitable exercise of the power to determine which first degree murder shall live and which shall die." *Wooden v. North Carolina,* 428 U.S. 280.

Finally, the Court observed that the North Carolina statute "treats all persons convicted of a designated offense not as uniquely individual human beings, but as members of a faceless, undifferentiated mass to be subjected to the blind infliction of the penalty of death." The Louisiana mandatory death penalty for first-degree murder suffered from similar inadequacies.

As a result of either *Furman* or *Gregg,* or both, virtually every state capital punishment statute had to be rewritten to provide flexible guidelines for judges and juries so that they may fairly decide capital cases and consider, and impose, if necessary, the death penalty.

A synthesis of these decisions provides the following basic outline of the probable state of the law currently:

(1) The death penalty is only constitutional if it is imposed after a separate sentencing hearing (which is itself subsequent to conviction for a capital crime) at which the aggravating and mitigating features of each particular case are considered. Such features relate not only to the offense but also to the character of the offender.

54

(2) There must be legislative guidance over what are "aggravating and mitigating" circumstances for the process of determining a sentence.

(3) The availability of review of this process on appeal must be specifically on appeal must be specifically provided for in the statute.

States that have enacted penalty laws since the 1976 decisions are: California, Delaware, Idaho, Illinois, Indiana, Kentucky, Louisiana, Maryland, Mississippi, Missouri, Montana, Nevada, New Hampshire, North Carolina, Oklahoma, South Carolina, Tennessee, Utah, Virginia, Washington and Wyoming.

States that enacted death penalty laws after the 1972 decision but before the 1976 decisions were: Alabama, Arizona, Arkansas, Colorado, Connecticut, Florida, Georgia, Nebraska, Ohio and Texas.

States with death penalty laws which have been held unconstitutional and therefore invalid are: New Jersey, New Mexico, New York, Pennslyvania, Rhode Island.

State that have no death penalty laws in force are: Alaska, Hawaii, Kansas, Iowa, Massachusetts, Maine, Michigan, Minnesota, North Dakota, Oregon, South Dakota, West Virginia and Wisconsin.

There is no death penalty in the territories of Guam, Puerto Rico, U.S. Virgin Islands or the District of Columbia. The Uniform Code of Military Justice retains the death penalty.

A dividend Supreme Court ruled 5-4 in *Everhart v. Georgia* and *Coker v. Georgia,* 97 S. Ct. 2861 (1977), that "rape is without doubt deserving of serious punishment, but in terms of moral depravity and of the injury to the person and to the public, it does not involve the unjustified taking of human life. . . . The murderer kills; the rapist, if no more that that, does not. Life is over for the victim of the murderers; for the rape victim, life may not be nearly so happy as it was, but it is not over and normally is not beyond repair. We have the abiding conviction that the death penalty, which is unique in its severity and revocability . . . . is an excessive penalty for the rapist who, as such, does not take human life."

The Court also held that kidnapping did not warrant the death penalty. This leaves only the taking of human life and treason (the death penalty for which *Everheart* raises serious questions) justifiable grounds for the imposition of the death penalty.

Inadequate consideration of mitigating circumstances is another ground on which the Court has invalidated state death penalties. Sandra Lockett was convicted for helping to plan and then driving the getaway car for a pawnshop robbery. Although it was unplanned, the owner of the pawnshop was murdered. Lockett also hid her accomplices in her home. Later, she was tried for capital murder of the pawnshop owner. According to the death penalty statute, the capital punishment had to be imposed on Lockett unless "(1) the victim induced or facilitated the offense; (2) it is unlikely that the offense would have been committed but for the fact that the offender was under duress, coercion, or strong provocation; or (3) the offense was primarily the product of the offender's psychosis or mental deficiency." Lockett was found guilty and sentenced to die. She appealed claiming that the Ohio law did not give the "sentencing judge a full opportunity to consider mitigating circumstances." Chief Justice Burger commented that "A statute that prevents the sentencer in capital cases from giving independent mitigating weights to aspects of the defendant's character and record to the circumstances of the offense proffered in mitigation creates the risk that the death penalty will be imposed in spite of factors that may call for a less severe penalty, and when the choice is between life and death, such risk is unacceptable and incompatible with the commands of the Eighth and Fourteenth Amendments." Since the Ohio statute did not permit and adequate consideration of mitigating circumstances, that part of it was found unconstitutional. On the same day, the Court invalidated a similar Arizona law in *Jordan v. Arizona*, 438 U.S. 911.

In *Witherspoon v. Illinois*, 391 U.S. 510 (1967), the Supreme Court found unconstitutional the simple exclusion of all who opposed the death penalty without trying to determine whether "their scruples would invariably compel them to vote against capital punishment." Such a selective process which eliminated all prospective jurors who opposed capital punishment would create a jury which "can speak only for a district and dwindling minority." It would not represent the community and would not be fair and impartial. "No defendant," concluded the Court, "can constructively be put to death at the hands of a tribunal so selected. . . . The state has stacked the deck against the (defendant). To execute this death sentence would deprive him of his life without due process of law."

But the findings in *Witherspoon* did not mean that no one opposing the death penalty could be excluded. A prospective juror had to be willing to "be willing to *consider* all the penalties provided by state law, and that he not be irrevocably committed before the trial has begun, to vote against the death penalty regardless of the facts and circumstances that might emerge in the course of proceedings." The Court indicated that the court could exclude for cause jurors "who made unmistakably clear (1) that they would *automatically* vote against the imposition of capital publishment without regard to any evidence that might be developed at the trial. . . or (2) that their attitudes toward the death penalty would prevent them from making an impartial decision as the defendant's *guilt*.

Finally, the Courted noted that based upon "presently available knowledge" that "We cannot simply conclude. . . that the exclusion of jurors opposed to capital punishment results in an unrepresentative jury on the issue of guilt or substantially increase the risk of conviction."

As a result of *Witherspoon,* it has become practice in most states, including Illinois, to exclude prospective jurors who indicate that they could not possibly, in good conscience, return a death penalty, from juries which will try capital cases.

Can a minor be sentenced to death? Upon being pulled over by a police officer, Eddings told his companions that if the "mother . . . pig tried to stop him he was going to blow him away." Eddings carried the threat, was convicted of first degree murder for killing a police officer and was sentenced to death. At the time of the murder, he was 16 years old, but nonetheless, was tried as an adult. At the sentencing hearing following the conviction, Eddings' lawyer presented substantial evidence of a turbulent family history, beatings by a harsh father, and serious emotional disturbance. The judge refused, *as a matter of law,* to consider in mitigation the circumstances of petitioner's unhappy upbringing and emotional disturbance, and found that the only mitigating circumstances was the petitioner's youth which was held to be insufficient to outweigh the aggravating circumstances.

Referring to *Lockett v. Ohio,* the Court, 5-4, ordered the sentence vacated because nothing could or should be precluded from considering *as a matter of law* as a mitigating factor. After consideration, such factors could be dismissed as insufficient, but all mitigating circumstances had to be considered. By implication, since the majority did not reverse the case on the issue of age, it let stand Oklahoma's decision to try him as an adult. Meanwhile, the dissenters, led by C.J. Burger, who filed the dissenting opinion in which Justices White, Blackmun, and Rehnquist joined, indicated that "there comes a time in every case when a court must 'bite the bullet." The Chief Justice observed that "The Court stops far short of suggesting that there is any constitutional proscription against the imposition of the death penalty on a person who was under age 18 when the murder was committed." Hence, while the Supreme Court did not directly rule on the question of minors being sentenced to death, the sense of the Court would appear to be that it would uphold such a sentencing.

Chapter 7

LEADING CRIMINAL LAW SUPREME COURT CASES SUMMARIES

Ableman v. Booth, 21 How. 506. A case involving a State's attempt to release an abolitionist editor held by a federal marshal for violating a federal law. Held, that when a person is legally in federal custody for a federal offence and this fact has been made known to State authorities by proper return on a writ of habeas corpus, the State is barred from proceeding further, federal authority being exclusive.

Adams v. New York, 192 U.S. 585, 48 L. Ed. 575. 24 S. Ct. 372 (1904). Refused to explicitly overrule the *Boyd* holding (See *Boyd v. U.S.*), but the Court limited that decision to the facts in the case. Hence, for all practical purposes the Court, returned to the common-law rule of admissibility on search and seizure.

Adams v. Williams, 407 U.S. 143, 32 L. Ed. 2d, 612, 92 S. Ct. 1921 (1972). A known informer's tip is sufficient to support a stop-and-frisk. Acting on a tip supplied moments earlier, about 2:15 A.M., in a high crime area, by an informant known to him, a police officer asked Williams to open his car door. Williams lowered the window, and the officer reached into the car and found a loaded handgun (which had not been visible from the outside). In Williams' waistband, precisely where the informant said it would be. Williams was arrested for unlawful possession of the handgun. A search incident to the arrest disclosed heroin on Williams' person (as the informant had reported) as well as other contraband.

Adamson v. California, 353 U.S. 46, 91 L. Ed. 1903, 67 S. Ct. 1672 (1947). Held, that a state constitutional provision, or statute, that allows the prosecutor or the court to comment on the failure of a defendant to testify is not unconstitutional as an abridgement of his privilege against self-incrimination under the Fifth and Fourteenth Amendments. This case reiterates earlier rulings that the due-process clause of the Fourteenth Amendment does not extend to State courts the procedural limitations of the first eight amendments.

Ashcraft v. Tennessee, 322 U.S. 143, 88 L. Ed. 1192, 64 S. Ct. 921 (1944). Held, that a confession obtained *under aggravating circumstances* (inherent coercion), coupled with unnecessary delays in arraignment, is involuntary, and inadmissible in a state court under due process of the Fourteenth Amendment Thus the Court coined the "inherently coercive" rule as a substantial equivalent of the "civilized standards" rule that had been created in *McNabb.*

Berger v. New York, 388 U.S. 41, 18 L. Ed. 2d 1040, 87 S. Ct. 1873 (1967). Held, New York State's permissive wiretap statute to be "too broad in its sweep resulting in a trespassory intrusion into a constitutionally protected area and is, therefore, violative of the Fourth and Fourteenth Amendments" The Court pointed out that since *Mapp (1961),* "the Fourth Amendment's right of privacy has been declared enforceable against the States through the Due Process Clause of the Fourteenth Amendment." The decision did not outlaw wiretapping. It only struck down New York's permissive wiretap statute as unconstitutional.

Brady v. U.S. 397 U.S. (1970) (together with *McMann v. Richardson, 397* 397 U.S. 759, and *Parker v. North Carolina,* 397 U.S. 790). The decisions in these three cases on guilty pleas in the same term of the Supreme Court attach paramount significance to the presence of counsel for the defendant during the pleading process.

This is a fine review of the plea of guilty as a rational choice over going to trial in certain instances.

Brown v. Illinois, 45 L. Ed. 2d, 416, 95 S. Ct. 2254 (1975). Held, that the mere giving of the warnings required by *Miranda v. arizona,* 384 U.S. 436, does not dissipate the taint of a defendant's illegal arrest and render admissible statements given after the arrest.

Brown v. Mississippi, 297 U.S. 278, 80 L. Ed. 682, 56 S. Ct. 461 (1936). In this first state-confession case to go to the Supreme Court of the United States, the Court held that the use by the State of an obviously coerced confession violated the petitioner's due process rights under the Fourteenth Amendment.

Burton v. United States, 391 U.S. 123, 20 L. Ed. 2d 476, 88 S. Ct. 1620 (1968). Held, that a confession of one defendant cannot be used at a joint trial in which it might prejudice a codefendant ("Because of the substantial risk that the jury, despite instructions to the contrary, looked to the incriminating extra-judicial statements in determining petitioner's guilt, admission of Evan's confession in this joint trial violated petitioner's right to cross examination secured by the Confrontation Clause of the Sixth Amendment.

Cady v. Dombrowski, 413 U.S. 433, 37 L. Ed. 2d 706, 93 S. Ct. 2523. Distinguishes between the search of a home and the search of an automobile, and allows more latitude in respect to the search of an automobile. "Where, as here, the trunk of an automobile, which the officers reasonably believed to contain a gun was vulnerable to intrusion by, we hold that the search was not 'unreasonable' within the meaning of the Fourth and Fourteenth Amendments.

California v. Byers, 402 U.S. 424, 29 L. Ed. 2d 9, 91 S. Ct. 1535 (1971). Held, that the Fifth Amendment's self incrimination clause neither vitiates a California statute that requires a motorist involved in an accident to stop and identify himself nor requires a restriction on the prosecutorial use of the information that the statute compels a motorist to supply.

Camera v. Municipal Court, 387 U.S. 523, 18 L. Ed. 2d 930, 87 S. Ct. 1727 (1967). Held, that health and fire inspectors are no longer entitled to search a home or business without warrant or consent.

Carroll v. United States, 267 U.S. 132, 69 L. Ed. 543, 45 S. Ct. 280 (1925). Held, that a moving vehicle can be stopped, and searched on probable cause that at the time it is carrying contraband or other illegally possessed goods. The Chief Justice brought out that there "is a necessary difference between a search of a store, dwelling house, or other structure in respect to which a proper official warrant readily may be obtained, and a search of ship, motor boat, wagon, or automobile, for contraband goods, where it is not practical to secure a warrant because the vehicle can be quickly moved out of the locality or jurisdiction in which the warrant must be sought."

Coleman v. Alabama, 399 U.S. 1, 26 L. Ed. 387, 90 S. Ct. 1999 (1970). Mr. Justice Brennan's principal opinion, in a case in which the defendant had been charged with assault with intent to murder, held that a preliminary hearing, if held, is a "critical stage," and an indigent defendant has a constitutional right to the appointment of counsel under the Sixth and Fourteenth Amendments.

Davis v. Mississippi, 394 384. U.S. 737, 16 L. Ed. 2d 895, 86 S. Ct. 1761 (1966). A landmark case holding that fingerprints taken as a result of an illegal arrest were inadmissible in evidence.

Elkins v. United States, 364 U.S. 206, 4 L. Ed. 2d 1169, 80 S. Ct. 1437; *Rios v. United States,* 364 U.S. 253, 4 L.

Ed. 2d 1688, 80 S. Ct. 1431 (1960). Overturned the so-called "silver platter" doctrine: the rule that evidence of crime which state police come upon in the course of an illegal search for a state crime may be turned over to federal authorities so long as federal agents did not participate in the search but simply received the evidence on a "silver platter."

Escobedo v. Illinois, 378 U.S. 478, 12 L. Ed. 2d 977, 84 S. Ct. 1758 (1964). "We hold only," the Court concluded, "that when the process shifts from investigatory to accusatory and its purpose is to elicit a confession, our adversary system begins to operate, and, under the circumstances here, the accused must be permitted to consult with his lawyer." The construction of the bridge that led to *Miranda v. Arizona* was begun in *Gideon v. Wainwright,* 372 U.S. 335 (1963), and completed in *Escobedo.*/

Foster v. California, 394 U.S. 440, 22 L. Ed. 2d 402, 89 S. Ct. 1127 (1969). Held, that what the police officers did in conducting the line-ups was "so unnecesarily suggestive and conductive to irreparable mistaken identification as to be a denial of due process under the Fourteenth Amendment." the opinion points up how not to conduct a line-up.

Furman v. Georgia, 408 U.S. 238, 92 S. Ct. 2726, 33 L. Ed. 2d 346 (1972). Held, in relating to the existing death penalties in Georgia and Texas, that "the imposition and carrying out of the death penalty in these cases constitutes cruel and unusual punishment in violation of the Eighth and Fourteenth Amendments." Although the decision effectively invalidated all death penalties as they were then applied, nine opinions were written resulting in confusion as to what, if any, conditions would render the death penalty valid.

Gerstein v. Pugh, 420 U.S. 103, 43 L. Ed. 2d 541, 95 S. Ct. 854 (1957). Held, that the Fourth Amendment requires a judicial determination of probable cause for pretrial restraint of liberty. The Court rejected contention that the prosecutor's decision to proceed by information was enough to satisfy the constitutional requirements.

Gideon v. Wainwright, 372 U.S. 335 (1963). A case in which the Court included among the fundamental rights of persons guaranteed by the Fourteenth Amendment the right under the Sixth Amendment to be represented by counsel when a person is being tried for a crime in a State court, including the right of an indigent defendant to have counsel assigned by the court.

Ginzberg v. United States, Held, that publications created and advertised solely in order to appeal to purient interests in sex had the characteristics of illicit merchandise and could not claim the protection of freedom of the press, though in a different context (as by sale to physicians) their distribution might not be challenged.

Gitlow v. New York, 268 U.S. 652, 69 L. Ed. 1138, 45 S. Ct. 625 (1925). Upheld the validity of New York's criminal anarchy act of 1902. The left-wing members of the Socialist Party met in convention in New York Cirt, June 21-24, 1919. The convention delegates instructed its executive committee to draft and publish the *Left Wing Manifesto* and adopted *Revolutionary Age* as the left wing's official newspaper. The *Manifesto* appeared in the July 5, 1919 issue of the *Revolutionary Age* and furnished the basis for the conviction of its business manager, Benjamin Gitlow, of criminal anarchy in New York.

Harris v. New York, 401 U.S. 222, 28 L. Ed. 2d 1, 91 S. Ct. 643 (1971). Held, that a prosecutor may use illegally obtained confession to prove that a defendant who testifies is lying.

Haynes v. Washington, 373 U.S. 503, 10 L. Ed. 2d 513, 83 S. Ct. 1336 (1963). Held, that when a confession is "obtained in an atmosphere of substantial coercion and inducements created by statements and actions of state authorities, it is inadmissible under due process of the Fourteenth Amendment." The police "coercion" in this case rested on their refusal to permit the prisoner to contact his wife unless he confessed, and kept him in a technically incommunicado status, even though there was very little to indicate that his statement in fact was unreliable. The Court expressly recognized at that time, the need for custodial interrogation. "Certainly, we do not mean to suggest that all interrogation of witnesses and suspects is impermissible."

In re Gault, 387 U.S. 1, 18 L. Ed. 2d 527, 87 S. Ct. 1428 (1967). Held, that the due process clause of the Fourteenth Amendment applies to proceedings in state juvenile courts to adjudicate a juvenile delinquent. The Court indicates that a juvenile is entitled, in the adjudicatory of a juvenile court proceeding, to substantially the same rights that are accorded to an adult in a criminal court. A wide divergence of views have been expressed by legal commentators and juvenile court personnel as to what *Gault* means, and its prospective reach on juvenile courts. But it has resulted in a complete alteration of the nation's juvenile court system.

In re Winship, 397 U.S. 358, 25 L. ed. 2d 368, Held, that the Due Process Clause, requires that the conviction of a criminally accused be based upon proof of guilt beyond a reasonable doubt; the same standard applies to the adjudicatory stage of a juvenile delinquency proceeding in which a youth is charged with an act that would constitute a crime if committed by an adult.

Irvine v. California, 347 U.S. 128, 98 L. Ed. 561, 74 S. Ct. 381 (1954). Held, that the exclusion of illegally seized evidence from a state proceeding was not required by due process of law, no matter how shocking the violation, so long as there was no element of physical coercion.

Kastigar et al. v. United States, 406 U.S. 441 32 L. Ed. 2d 212, 92 S. Ct. 1653 (1972). Upholds the limited immunity the Organized Crime Control Act of 1970 gives witnesses who are compelled to testify before grand juries. "Transactional immunity would afford broader prorection than the Fifth Amendment privilege, and is not constitutionallly required," the Court declared. The federal law had been copied by several states.

Kerby v. California, 374 U.S. 23, 10 L. Ed. 2d 276, 83 S. Ct. 1623 (1963). In the first state case to reach the Court after *Mapp,* dealing with *Mapp's* implication, held, that searches by state police must conform to federal standards of reasonableness. Further, held, that "States are not precluded from developing workable rules governing arrests, searches, and seizures to meet the practical demands of effective criminal investigation in the states. . . ."

Kirby v. Illinois, Held, that the formal charge, preliminary hearing, indictment, information, or arraignment, is the cutoff point when a person is entitled to have counsel present at a line-up.

Lopez v. United States, 373 U.S. 427, 10 L. Ed. 2d 462, 83 S. Ct. 1381. Held, that the Fourth Amendment did not apply in the absence of a physical trespass when incriminating statements were obtained by an electronic listening device Agent of the IRS had a recording on his person by means of which the defendant's incriminating statements were recorded.

Louisiana v. ex. rel. Francis v. Resweber, 329 U.S. 459
(1947). A case in which a convicted murder who had
escaped death due to mechanical failure of the electric
chair sought to prevent a second attempt at execution
on the grounds of double jeopardy and cruel and
unusual punishment. Held, that Louisiana was not
violating these standards is proceeding a second time
to carry out death by electrocution.

Mallory v. United States, 354 U.S. 449 (1957). Held, that
a confession, obtained from a defendant while being
detained by arresting officers for an unnecessarily long
time (about 8 hours) before being brought before a
committing magistrate, was invalid as evidence in a
subsequent trial. *Cf. Escobedo v. Illinois, Miranda v.
Arizona.*

Malloy v. Hogan, 378 U.S. 1. 12 L. Ed. 2d 653, 84 S. Ct.
1489 (1964). Held, that the States, the same as the
United States, cannot compel incriminating testimony-
thus overruling *Adamson v. California, infra.* This
decision makes the self-incrimination privilege of the
Fifth Amendment applicable to the States through the
due process clause of the Fourteenth Amendment.

Mapp v. Ohio, 367 U.S. 643, L. Ed. 2d 1081, 81 S. Ct.
1681 (1961). Held, that the Fourth Amendment is
applicable to the States through the due process clause
of the Fourteenth Amendment.

Massiah v. United States, 377 U.S. 201, 12 L. Ed. 2d 246,
84 S. Ct. 1199 (1964). Held, that no indicated defendant
can be interrogated under any circumstances in the
absence of his attorney without having his Sixth
Amendment right to counsel impaired. A brief *per
curiam* opinion made the *Massiah* doctrine binding on
the states under the Fourteenth Amendment. *McLeod
v. Ohio,* 381 U.S. 356 (1965).

McGautha v. California, 402 U.S. 1983 (1871). This is a

controlling case on whether the death penalty can be imposed without standards to govern its imposition (due process). It discusses the role of the penalty jury in capital cases and holds that the Constitution requires no more than that trials be fairly conducted and that guaranteed rights of defendants be scrupulously respected.

McKiever v. Pennsylvania (In re Barbara Burns et al.), 403 U.S. 528, 29 L. Ed. 2d 647, 91 S. Ct. 1976 (1971). Held, that the Sixth Amendment does not require trial by jury in State juvenile delinquency proceedings.

McNabb v. United States, 318 U.S. 332, 87 L. Ed. 819, 63 S. Ct. 708 (1943). Held, that a confession that had been obtained while the suspect was illegally detained under aggravated circumstances- failure to arraign promptly coupled with noncoercive police methods- was inadmissible in a federal court.

Mempha v. Rhay, 398 U.S. 128 (1967). In this case, dealing with revocation of probation, the Court affirmed the right to counsel, "at every stage of a criminal proceeding where substantial rights of a criminal accused may be affected." If the accused in probation revocation proceedings is indigent, counsel must be provided for him.

Michigan v. Tucker, 417 U.S. 433, 41 L. Ed. 2d 182, 94 S. Ct. 2357 (1974). Held, a witness's testimony against defendant's interest (held not to be the fruits of the poisonous tree) is admissible even though a statement made by the defendant without full *Miranda* warnings led by the police to the witness.

Miranda v. Arizona, 384 U.S. 436, 16 L. Ed. 2d 694, 86 S. Ct. 1602 (1966). Imposed upon law enforcement officials a scheme of preinterrogation warnings and advice as federal constitutional prerequisites to the admissibility of confessions and statements in State and federal prosecutions. The court expressly held that the privilege against self-incrimination is available outside of criminal court proceedings and applied to police interrogations of persons "in custody."

Murphy v. Waterfront Commission, 378 U.S. 52, 12 L. Ed. 2d 678. 84 S. Ct. 1594 (1964). Held, that the constitutional privilege against self incrimination protects a State witness against incrimination under federal as well as state law and a federal witness against incrimination under state law- thus overruling *United States v. Murdock,* 284 U.S. 41.

Olmstead v. United States, Held, that messages passing over telephone wires were not within the protection of the Fourth Amendment, and, for this reason, the Amendment did not apply as there was no physical trespass on premises owned or under the control of the defendant.

Oregon v. Hass, 419 U.S. 823, 43 L. ed 2d 570, 95 S. Ct. 1215 (1975). Held, that ". . .(T)he shield provided by *Miranda* is not to be perverted to a license to testify inconsistently, or even prejuriously, free from the risk of confrontation with prior inconsistent utterances."

Orozco v. Texas, 394 U.S. 324, 22 L. Ed. 2d 311, 89 S. Ct. 1095, held, that once an accused is in custody, regardless of where he is in custody, *Miranda* warnings must be given if a statement, or evidence therefrom, is to be admissible.

Palko v. Connecticut, 302 U.S. 319 (1937). Held, that the prohibition of double jeopardy applicable to U.S. courts under the Fifth Amendment, is not included among the procedural limitations enforceable against State courts under the due-process clause of the Fourteenth Amendment. The test of the applicability of procedural rights secured by that clause is never a formal one but, in the words of Justice Cardozo,

71

depends on whether or not the action against a defendant is "so acute and shocking that our polity will not endure it."

Robinson v. California, 370 U.S. 660, 82 S. Ct. 1417, 8 L. Ed. 758 (1962). Held, that the Eighth Amendment barring cruel and unusual punishment, was applicable to the individual punishment, was applicable to the individual states. This is the first instance of its application to the states.

Schmerber v. California, 384 U.S. 757, 16 L. Ed. 2d 908, 86 S. Ct. 1826 (1966). Held, that the prosecution can use as evidence in a drunken driving test the analysis of a blood sample taken without the consent of the accused without violating his Fifth, Sixth and Fourteenth Amendment rights against self-incrimination. The Court distinguishes between the production of compelled physical evidence, and testimonial compulsion, i.e., words produced by someone's lips.

Schneckloth v. Bustamonte, 412 U.S. 218, 36 L. Ed. 2d 854, 93 S. Ct. 2041 (1973). Held, that warnings are unnecessary as prerequisite to a consent search in a noncustodial situation.

Sheppard v. Maxwell, 384 U.S. 333 (1966). This decision contains an extensive discussion of the effect of unfair distorted publicity upon the jurors at the time of trial, Decision notes that neither prosecutors, counsel for defense the accused, witness, court staff, or enforcement officers coming under the jurisdiction of the trial court should be permitted to frustrate its functions by actions or statements threatening the fair trial of the defendant.

Unger v. Sarafite, 376 U.S. 575 (1964). Held that there was not violation of due process where the same judge presided at the trial and the contempt hearing of a witness openly critical of judicial control of the trial, despite the fact that a request for a continuance was refused and the offender permitted only five days to prepare for a defense.

United States v. Wade, 338 U.S. 218, 18 L. Ed. 2d 1149, 87 S. Ct. 1926 (1967). Held, that police line-ups constitute a critical stage of the prosecutorial process, and the Sixth Amendment right to counsel attaches at that time, applicable to the states through due process of the Fourteenth Amendment.

Warden v. Hayden, 387 U.S. 294, 18 L. Ed. 2d 782, 87 S. Ct. 1642 (1967). Held, that officials may use as evidence in courts items such as clothing seized by the police in lawful searches of the residences of suspects. The Court, in short, abrogated the "mere evidence" rule. This decision shows a "shift" in Fourth Amendment emphasus from property to privacy and redounds to the benefit of law enforcement officials as well as their quarry. The police can seize more things, but an accused can challenge more kinds of evil.

RECENT DECISIONS OF THE SUPREME COURT

Bearden v. Georgia, 461 U.S. 103 S. Ct. 2064 (1983). Held, that revoking probation and imprisoning a person because he cannot pay a fine without considering the reasons for the inability to pay or determining whether alternative methods of punishment would satisfy the state's penal interest were contrary to the due process clause.

Pulley v. Harris, 465 U.S., 104 S. Ct. 871 (1984). Held, that a capital sentence can be imposed even though no state reviewing court compares the sentence in the particular defendant's case with the sentences imposed by the state's court in similar cases. Such review, in the opinion of the majority, may help to avoid arbitrary

imposition of the death penalty. But the Federal
Constitution requires only that there be adequate
statutory controls over the discretion which can be
exercised by the jury. Upon consideration, the Court
determined that such controls were present in the
California statutory scheme.

Mabry v. Johnson, 104 S. Ct. 2543 (1984). Held, that a
defendant is not entitled to specific performance of a
plea offer which has been withdrawn before he has
acted to his own detriment in reliance upon such offer.
In the Court's view, a plea agreement, which is simply
executory and anticipatory in character, does not
affect a defendant's liberty or other substantial interest;
instead, it is the plea of guilty in response to such
agreement which results in a deprivation of liberty or
other adverse consequence.

Schall v. Martin, 467 U.S., 104 S. Ct. 2403 (1983). The
New York statute at issue authorizes preventive detention of juveniles accused of delinquency if the court
makes a finding that there is a "serious risk" that prior
to the court hearing the child may commit an act that if
committed by an adult, would be a crime. The lower
Federal District Court had found that the Act was
administered for punitive purposes and violated due
process of law by imposing punishment for un-
adjudicated crimes. The Supreme Court disagreed,
finding that the statute satisfied due process requirements. It concluded that the statute and the detention
which it authorized were nonpunitive, and that pre-
detention procedural safeguards were adequate. The
Court also states that there is nothing inherently
unattainable about a prediction of future criminal
conduct.

Thigpen v. Roberts, 468 U.S., 104 S. Ct. 2916 (1984). In
1974 the Court held in *Blackledge v. Perry,* 417 U.S.

21, 94 S. Ct. 2098, that due process of law is violated when a prosecutor, in order to penalize or deter defense appeals files an enhanced charge. In the present case the Court held that in a factual setting described as "identical" in its relevant facts, that the prosecutor's actions had raised a presumption of vindictiveness which the state had failed to rebut. In *Thigpen,* the defendant had been convicted of four traffic misdemeanors. Thereafter he appealed from the Justice of Peace Court in which the misdemeanors had been tried, to the Circuit Court, seeking a trial *de novo.* At that point, he was indicted for traffic manslaughter, a felony. The Court concluded that prosecution of the defendant for a felony, following his invocation of his statutory right to appeal his misdemeanor convictions, constituted an unconstitutional exercise of vindictive prosecution.

United States v. Gouveia, 104 S. Ct. 2292 (1984). Six defendants, all prison inmates suspected of killing a fellow inmate, were placed in administrative detention for prolonged periods before being indicted. The Circuit court held that their right to counsel had been denied by the prolonged detention and the failure to have appointed counsel at an earlier time. Court, reversed, holding that the Sixth Amendment right to counsel does not attach until the initiation of adversary proceedings against a defendant.

Richardson v. United States, 468 U.S., 104 S. Ct. 3081 (1984). Defendant had been charged in a three count indictment. At trial, the jury convicted on one count, but a mistrial was declared when the jurors could not reach a verdict on the other two counts. The defendant sought to avoid retrial on those counts by asserting the double jeopardy bar against reprosecution after acquittal. Court declined to uproot the settled doctrine that

75

no violation of the double jeopardy clause occurs upon a reprosecution following a hung jury.

Berkemer v. McCarty, 468 U.S., 104 S. Ct. 3138 (1984). Defendant had been arrested for drunk driving, a misdemeanor. He was questioned about his condition by the arresting officer, and admitted consuming two beers and recently smoking "several joints of marijuana." Because he was not given the *Miranda* warnings before being questioned, he sought, albeit unsuccessfully, to suppress his incriminating responses. Held, that he had been entitled to the warnings. Focus of the Court's opinion was the consideration that the defendant, though stopped only for a misdemeanor, was, nonetheless, indisputably in custody.

California v. Beheler, 103 S. Ct. 3517 (1983). Defendant called the police after a shooting, and he agreed later to go to the station house. After a brief interview, he was allowed to leave. Held, that his motion to suppress his statements did not require a *Miranda* warning because he had not been in custody when the statements were given to the officers.

Illinois v. Andreas, 463 U.S., 103 S. Ct. 3319 (1983). Held, that a controlled delivery of contraband, lawfully discovered in a closed container (which thereafter was closed again for delivery to the suspect), did not constitute a search. Customs officers discovered marijuana concealed in a large shipping trunk which had been forwarded to O'Hare Airport in Chicago from India. Following discovery of the contraband, the container was closed and arrangements were made to have the container delivered to the defendant's residence by other agents, who observed his receipt of the container.

Massachusetts v. Sheppard, 104 S. Ct. 342, L. Ed. 273 2d (1984). Held, that the exclusionary rule is inapplicable where the officer conducting the search acted in objectively reasonable reliance on a warrant issued by a detached and neutral magistrate that subsequently is determined to be invalid due to a technical error.

New York v. Quarles, 104 S. Ct. 2626, 81 L. Ed. 2550 2d (1984). Held, that when a police officer questions a suspect regarding a situation which poses a threat to public safety, the suspect's answers are admissible as evidence against him even though he was not given *Miranda* warnings prior to the questioning. The officer's subjective motivation for the questioning does not affect the admissibility of the suspect's answers.

Hobby v. United States, 104 S. Ct. 3093, 82 L. Ed. 2d 2260 (1984). Held, that discrimination in the under-representation of Negroes and women as foremen, does not require reversal of the conviction of a white male defendant and dismissal of the inductment against him.

United States v. Leon, 104 S. Ct. 3405, 82 L. Ed. 2d 677 (1984). Held, that evidence obtained by police officers in "objectively reasonable" reliance on a search warrant issued by a neutral and detached magistrate need not be excluded from the prosecution case-in-chief.

Michigan v. Clifford, 104 S. Ct. 641, 78 L. Ed. 2d 477 91984). Held, absent exigent circumstances or consent, fire officials are required to obtain an administrative search warrant to investigate the cause of a fire. A search to gather evidence of arson requires that a criminal search warrant be obtained upon a showing of probable cause.

United States v. Karo, 104 S. Ct. 3296, 82 L. Ed. 2d 530 (1984). Held, the monitoring of an electronic beeper in a private residence violated the Fourth Amendment rights of those who have a justifiable interest in the privacy of the residence.

Oliver v. United States, 104 S. Ct. 1735, 80 L. Ed. 2d 2214 (1984). Held, the open fields doctrine permits law enforcement officers to search private land for marijuana fields despite the presence of "No Trespass" signs and lack of public access to the fields.

Immigration and Naturalization Service v. Delgado, 104 S. Ct. 1758 (1984). Held, no detentions had taken place in the following set of facts: INS agents had conducted surveys of factories believed to be employing illegal aliens. Agents were stationed at entrances while other agents questioned many of the workers, asking them to produce identification. Lower court had held that the manner in which the operations had been undertaken amounted to a seizure of the entire workforce at each location. The Supreme Court, in disagreeing, noted that it had not previously determined whether mere questioning of an individual could amount to a seizure. Its earlier decisions, the Court concluded, make clear that police questioning, without more, is unlikely to result in a Fourth Amendment violation. If an individual refuses to respond, and the officers take additional steps, then, the Court stated, the officers must possess some minimal level of objective justification to validate the detention or seizure. In *Delgado,* the questioning by the agents was nothing more than a brief encounter.

GLOSSARY OF CRIMINAL LAW TERMINOLOGY

abandonment - The discontinuation of a planned and intended crime before its actual commission.

abduction - The common-law crime of taking a female person (wife, child, or ward) away without her consent by the use of persuasion, fraud, or violence, for the purpose of marriage, prostitution, or defilement. *See also kidnapping.*

abet - To knowingly facilitate the commission or attempted commission of a crime. *See also accessory; aid and abet; conspiracy.*

ab initio - ("from the beginning") Null and void because of fatal defects at the time an agreement was made (as, in criminal law, an illegal plea bargain).

abscond - To flee or conceal oneself in order to avoid legal proceedings (as to jump bail); also to flee with the property of another, as when a bank teller absconds with the funds entrusted to him.

accusation - A formal or informal statement charging a person, persons, or corporation with having committed a crime. The formal accusation can be made as an information or an indictment.

acquit - To find not guilty.

acquittal - A verdict of not guilty in a criminal trial.

actus reus - The criminal act, as contrasted with *men rea,* the criminal intent.

Admission - An acknowledgment by either prosecution or defense that a statement of fact made by the opposing side is true.

Aid and abet - To assist in the commission of a crime of words, act, encouragement, or support.

Alibi - A contention of a defendant that he was in another place at the time of the commission of the criminal act of which he is accused, and hence could not have done what he is charged with doing; also, a lay term for excuse.

Alibi, notice of - Information that the defense is required to give to the prosecution before a trial if a defense of alibi will be made, that is, if the defense will contend that the accused was elsewhere at the time of the crime. Such a notice is necessary so that the prosecution may investigate before the trial and be prepared for cross-examination and rebuttal.

Allegation - An assertion of the facts which a party to an action expects to prove; in a criminal trial, the charge or indictment.

Alias - Any name used for an official purpose that is different from a person's legal name.

Appeal - Review of the trial record by a higher court to determine whether errors of law or procedure justify reversal of conviction.

Appellant - The person who contests the correctness of a court order, judgment, or other decision and who seeks review and relief in a court having appellate jurisdiction, or the person in whose behalf this is done.

Arraignment - The formal reading of charges against a defendant and the entry of his plea; presided over by an arraignment judge.

Arrest - The act of taking a person into custody for the purpose of answering a criminal charge.

Arrest, citizen's - The arrest, without a warrant, of an alleged offender by a person who is not a law enforcement officer, for a felony or a breach of the peace committed in the latter's presence.

Attempt - An act done with intent to commit a crime but falling short of its actual commitment.

Autopsy - A postmortem medical examination, usually mandatory if death result from other than natural causes.

Bailiff - The court officer whose duties are to keep order in court room and to maintain physical custody of jury.

Bench warrant - A document issued by a court directing that a law enforcement officer bring the person named therein before the court; usually one who has failed to obey a court order to notice to appear.

Bifurcated trial - In criminal proceedings, a special two-part trial proceeding in which the issue of guilt is tried in the first step, and if a conviction results, the appropriate sentence or applicable sentencing statute is determined in the second step.

Bill of Particulars - A detailed statement of the allegations at issue in a legal proceeding.

Burden of proof - The requirement that one side in an adversary hearing establish with affirmative proof its position on a point of contention.

Calendar - A listing of pending cases and the date and place of the next step in their processing; a listing of all cases in any one court for a given day.

Capital crime (capital offense) - Any felony for which capital punishment is permitted.

Capital punishment - The death penalty; execution as punishment for a crime.

Career criminal - In prosecutorical and law enforcement usage, a person having a past record of multiple arrests or convictions for serious crimes, or an usually large number of arrests or convictions for crimes of varying degrees of seriousness.

Causation - The relationship that must be established to hold a person responsible for a consequence of his action.

Certiorari - The transference of an action from an inferior to a superior court for review; the process is initiated by a writ of certiorari.

Challenge - An objection, usually regarding a specific prospective juror, made to the judge by a party to a case, requesting that the person in question not be allowed to serve on the jury. The challenge may be for cause or peremptory. The defendant in a court-martial may challenge a member of the court for cause.

Challenge, peremptory - A challenge to a prospective juror made without stating a reason or cause. A limited number of such challenges may be made by both defense and prosection.

Challenge for cause - A challenge to a prospective juror for a specific reason or cause.

Change of venue - The movement of a case from the jurisdiction of one court to that of another court which has the same subject matter jurisdiction authority but is in a different geographic location.

Charge - Facts or allegations pertaining to an accused in a complaint or indictment; also, the instructions given by the judge when he charges the jury-that is, when he informs it regarding the law and the alternative verdicts it may reach.

Citation - An order issued by a court or the police, commanding that the named person appear before the court on a certain date, usually to answer charges for a minor violation.

Civil death - The loss of numerous rights and privileges as a result of a sentence of death or life imprisonment. Such losses may include nullification of a marriage, distribution of an estate, or denial of the right to sue or be sued.

Civil disabilities - Rights or privileges denied a person as a result of conviction or a guilty plea, in addition to or other than the imposed legal penalty.

Clemency - The name given for the type of executive or legislative action where the severity of punishment of a single person or a group of persons is reduced or the punishment stopped, or a person is exempted from prosecution for certain actions.

Commit - To order into custody, either to a correctional facility or a mental institution.

Common law - The legal system in effect in the United States consisting of binding rules derived from custom and precedent as contrasted with those enacted into law by statute.

Competency to stand trial - The concept that a defendant should be tried only if he has sufficient ability at the time of trial to understand the proceedings against him, to consult with his lawyer with a reasonable degree of understanding, and to assist in his own defense.

Complainant - The victim of a crime, or someone acting for the victim (as a parent or guardian) who initiates the criminal justice process.

Complaint - The allegation that a crime or violation of law has been committed.

Computer crime - A popular name for crimes committed by use of a computer or crimes involving misuse or destruction of computer equipment or computerized information, sometimes specifically theft committed by means of manipulation of a computerized financial transaction system, or the use of computer services with intent to avoid payment.

Confession - A voluntary admission by a suspect of his involvement in one or more crimes. A coerced admission, when repudiated and retracted, would not qualify technically as a confession.

Confession, coerced - An admission of guilt secured by threat or use of force.

Confidence game - A popular name for false representation to obtain money or any other thing of value, where deception is accomplished through the trust placed by the victim in the character of the offender.

Consumer fraud - Deception of the public with respect to cost, quality, purity, safety, durability, performance effectiveness, dependability, availability and adequacy of choice relating to goods or services offered or furnished, and with respect to credit or other matters relating to terms of sales.

Contempt of court - Intentionally obstructing a court in the administration of justice, or acting in a way calculated to lessen its authority or dignity, or failing to obey its lawful orders.

Corporate crime - An illegal act or acts committed by a corporate body or by executives and managers acting on behalf of a corporation. Such acts include consumer fraud, price-fixing, and restraint of trade.

Corpus delicti - ("the body of the crime") The elements of a charge that must be proved to establish that the crime has occurred.

Count - Each separate offense charged against one or more persons, as listed in a complaint, indictment, or information.

Counterfeiting - Unauthorized reproduction of currency, medals, stamps, documents, or artwork, with the intention of fraudulently passing these to others as genuine.

Court, appellate - Any court that reviews a trial court's actions, or the decisions of another (but lower-level) appellate court, to determine whether errors have been made and to decide whether to uphold or overturn a verdict.

Crime of passion - Unpremeditated murder or assault, committed under circumstances of great anger, jealousy, or other emotional stress.

Criminal justice - The entire system of crime prevention

and detection, apprehension of suspects, arrest, trial, adjudication of guilt or innocence, and handling of the guilty by correctional agencies, together with the executive, legislative, and judicial rules governing these procedures and processes.

Criminal law - The body of legislation and judicial interpretations defining criminal acts (substantive criminal law), in contrast to laws specifying procedures for determination of guilt or innocence (procedural criminal law)

Criminal possession - Having on one's person or under one's effective control objects or substances illegally possessed, as guns or drugs. Criminal possession applies also to objects legally possessed when there is the intention of using them to commit a crime, as picks in burglary.

Culpability - Blameworthiness; responsibility in some sense for an event or situation deserving of moral blame.

Custody - Legal or physical control of a person or thing.

Deadly weapon - An instrument designed to inflict serious bodily injury or death, or capable of being used for such a purpose.

Driving under the influence - Unlawful operation of any motor vehicle while under the influence of alcohol or a controlled substance or drug.

Due process of law - A right guaranteed by the Fifth, Sixth, and Fourteenth Amendments of the United States Constitution, and generally understood, in legal contexes, to mean due course of legal proceedings, according to the rules and forms which have been established for the protection of private rights.

Entrapment - An arrangement made by police, or persons acting on behalf of the police, to induce, encourage, or instigate the commission of a crime that would not have been committed if it were not for the active intervention of the governmental agent and the desire to make an arrest. In defined circumstances it constitutes a defense.

Euthansia - Mercy killing, such as assisting in or hastening the death of a very old or terminally ill person, with or without his consent, or killing a malformed or mentally defective infant.

Evidence, circumstantial - Physical evidence from which judge and jury may infer facts. For example, a fingerprint on a gun is circumstantial evidence that the gun was handled by the suspect.

Evidence, corroborating - Evidence that confirms testimony previously admitted.

Evidence, exculpatory - Evidence that tends to clear an accused from blame or guilt, or from involvement in an offense. When such evidence is known to the prosecutor, it must be divulged to the court or to the defense.

Exclusionary rule - A rule that generally operates to exclude from admission at a criminal trial certain evidence, such as physical evidence, the defendant's confession, or identification by a witness, because it was obtained as a result of unlawful activities by law enforcement officers.

Extortion - Unlawfully obtaining or attempting to obtain something of value from another by compelling the other person to deliver it by the threat of eventual physical injury or other harm to that person or his property, or of a third person.

Extradition - The surrender by one state to another of an individual accused or convicted of an offense in the second state.

Fence - Receiver and seller of stolen goods.

Finding - A conclusion reached by a court on a matter of

fact, for example, that the defendant is or is not competent to stand trial.

Forensic - Relating to law, courts or the judiciary. For example, forensic science is the application of chemistry, physics or other sciences to the identification of physical evidence.

Forensic psychiatry - The application of psychiatric procedures in a legal setting to determine criminal responsibility, legal sanity or insanity, competency to stand trial, commitment to a mental facility, or related issues. Forensic psychiatry is concerned with psychiatric advice or opinion on a crime, a defendant, or a convicted offender.

Frisk - To search the clothing and property in the immediate possession of a suspect. A frisk is usually less intrusive than a full search of the kind permitted incident to a lawful arrest.

Fugitive - One who has escaped confinement or absconded from bail, probation, or parile; a deserter, a draft evader; one who flees a jurisdiction or goes into hiding to avoid arrest, indictment, or trial.

Good Samaritan - A person other than a police officer who is not directly involved in a crime but who steps in to prevent injury, aid a victim, or apprehend the criminal. The Good Samaritan is usually a bystander or passerby.

Graft - Coerced or voluntary payments made to influence public officials in their official conduct; for example, payments made to police to overlook an illegal activity such as prostitution.

Grand jury - A body of persons who have been selected according to law and sworn to hear the evidence against accused persons and determine whether there is sufficient evidence to bring those persons to trial, to investigate criminal activity generally, and to investigate the conduct of public agencies and officials.

Habeas corpus - ("you have the body") A writ or court order mandating that a warden, jailer, or other official holding a person in custody produce that person in court so that the legality of the confinement can be determined. Also resorted to in noncriminal actions, as in the determination of child custody, or a hearing on a patient's demand for release from a mental institution.

Hearsay - Inadmissible testimony by a witness as to what he heard or was told outside of court. Under special conditions, such hearsay as a dying declaration or a statement by an expert witness is admissible.

Hot pursuit (fresh pursuit) - Immediate, insight pursuit of an escaping felon that permits a police officer to epart from his jurisdiction or to intrude on private premises.

Ignorantia Legis non excusat - ("ignorance of the law is no excuse") The principle that an accused is not freed from criminal responsibility because he was unaware that his act was in violation of the law.

Immunity - Exemption from a duty or penalty contrary to the general rule, for example, immunity from prosecution of one who turns state's evidence, or immunity of public officials for their official acts.

Impeach - To discredit, particularly by challenging the truthfulness of a witness.

In camera - ("in a chamber") Criminal proceedings from which the media and the general public are barred, as in family and juvenile courts.

Incest - Illegal sexual activity between two persons closely related by blood or marriage.

Inchoate crime - Conduct made criminal even though it has not yet produced the harm that the law seeks to prevent.

Indictment - The formal written accusation submitted to

the court by a grand jury, alleging that a specified person(s) has committed a specified offense(s), usually a felony.

Information - A formal written accusation of a crime; it is different from an indictment in that it is issued by a prosecutor rather than a grand jury.

Insanity - (legal insanity) A defense based on the defendant's lack of responsibility at the time of the act owing to mental disease or defect.

Insanity - (temporary) Legal insanity which existed only at the time of the act.

Intent, criminal - (*mens rea*) The harboring of a plan, hope, or state of mind favorable to the commission of a crime.

Judicial notice - The right of the court to take note, without an offer of proof by either party, of facts known to a veritable certainty and available in sources of indisputable accuracy.

Jurisdiction - The territory, subject matter, or person over which the lawful authority may be exercised by a court or other justice agency, as determined by statute or constitution.

Jury, hung - A trial jury which, after exhaustive deliberation, cannot agree on a unanimous verdict, necessitating a mistrial.

Justification - The defense that an otherwise illegal act, particularly involving the use of force, is permitted because of such circumstances as self-defense or the necessity of using force for the purpose of making a lawful arrest.

Juvenile - A person who has not reached an age prescribed by law (generally eighteen). A juvenile is not routinely tried by a criminal court if he is accused of a crime, and he is ineligible for voting, military service, marriage, and the making of a binding contract until the prescribed age is reached.

Leniency - Punishing an offender less than is deserved or authorized.

Lesser included offense - A crime less grave than the one charged but not requiring a separate charge for a guilty verdict, because the less serious offense is automatically implied by the more serious one. For example, one charged with murder may also be found guilty of inflicting bodily harm.

Mistake of fact - A defense based on the grounds that a defendant did not know certain facts, that he could not have been expected to have known them, and that there could be no crime without such knowledge.

Mistake of law - A defense, rarely recognized, offered by an accused that he did not know his act was criminal or did not comprehend the legal consequences of what he was doing.

Mitigating circumstance - Any circumstance that is thought sufficient to diminish the degree of guilt and justify a more lenient sentence, while not excusing the misconduct of the accused.

M'Naghten rule - The rule laid down by the House of Lords after the 1843 verdict of "not guilty by reason of insanity" in the case of David M'Naghten. The rule stated that the perpetrator of a crime is not to be held criminally responsible, if, at the time of the act, he suffered from a disease of the mind either making him unable to know the nature of the act he was perpetrating or, if he did know it, making him unable to realize that what he was doing was wrong.

Necessity - The defense of justification of an otherwise criminal act on the ground that the perpetrator was compelled to commit it because a greater evil would have ensued had he failed to do so. Thus, one could plead necessity if he committed arson to destroy official documents that would otherwise have fallen into the hands of a wartime enemy.

Negligence, criminal - Conduct sufficiently careless to constitute the basis of a crime which result in death, injury, or damage to property, and which becomes subject to prosecution as a crime.

No-knock entry - Police procedure permitted in certain raids to avoid giving suspects time to destroy evidence, escape, or prepare to resist.

Omission - A failure to act that constitutes a crime when it involves nonperformance of an action the person is under duty to perform, imposed either by the criminal law (for example, to file income-tax returns) or by the civil law (for example, to provide necessities for one's children).

Original jurisdiction - The authority of a court to try a case at its beginning; this is the first court to which the case is brought for trial.

Overtact - An open act in furtherance of criminality (as opposed to an idea, a plan, or an omission) that may be necessary for a conviction of an uncompleted effort, a conspiracy, or treason.

Pardon - An act of clemency in which a crime allegedly committed by one found guilty is forgiven. A full pardon acts to annul a guilty verdict, restoring a defendant to a position of not having been convicted and of not being triable again for the same offense because of double-jeopardy protection.

Parole - The status of an offender conditionally released from a correctional institution before completion of his maximum prison sentence. A paroled offender is placed under the supervision of an authorized agency and subjected to restrictions, violation of which may result in revocation of parole.

Parricide - Killing of one's father, mother, or other close relative.

Plea - A defendant's formal answer in court to the charges brought against him in a complaint, information, or indictment.

Plea bargaining - (plea negotiating) Discussions between the prosecutor and the defense concerning the giving of some apparent concession (a lower sentence, a reduction in the seriousness of the charge, or a reduction in the number of charges) to the defendant in exchange for his waiver of trial and plea of guilty.

Prepronderance of the Evidence - The greater weight of the evidence presented by one side in an adversary proceeding. In a civil suit, a case is supposed to be decided by a fair prepronderance of the credible evidence. In a criminal proceeding this is insufficient, and a defendant can be found guilty only if the guilt is established beyond a reasonable doubt.

Presentment - A charge against an accused, issued by a grand jury. When such a charge is made by a grand jury upon submission of evidence by the prosecutor, it is known as an indictment; when made without request or submission of evidence by the prosecutor, it is a presentment.

Presumption of innocence - The principle that in a criminal case a defendant is innocent unless and until proved guilty. The burden of proof is always on the prosecution to demonstrate guilt, and never upon the defendant to demonstrate innocence.

Privileged communication - Information that may not be revealed in evidence over the objection of the person holding the privilege because it was communicated in the course of a special relationship, such as husband-wife, physician-patient, lawyer-client, or clergyman-penitent.

Probable cause - Reasonable grounds to believe that items legitimatly sought are located on a premises, thus justifying a search; or that person has committed a crime, thus justifying an arrest.

Punishment - Any pain or deprivation imposed on a person by sentence of a court or by a lawful administrative authority (such as a prison disciplinary officer) because that person has been judged guilty of a violation of the law.

Punishment, cruel and unusual - A phrase used in the Eighth Amendment to the U.S. Constitution but not defined with specifity by the Supreme Court; it generally refers to punishment for a given offense that is inflicted rarely, is excessively brutal, and is highly disproportionate to what is deserved for the crime committed.

Reasonable doubt - Lack of certainty as to the truth of a charge; belief that all other reasonable hypotheses, except that the defendant is guilty as charged, cannot be excluded. In a criminal case, a defendant can be found guilty only when no reasonable doubt exists in the minds of the jurors (or judge or judges, in a bench trial).

Rebuttal - The introduction of evidence contradicting or refuting adverse testimony; the effort to demonstrate that the adversary's witnesses are mistaken or lack credibility. The rebuttal is also the point in a trial at which such contradicting testimony is introduced.

Recidivist (repeater) - A habitual or career criminal; one who, having been convicted and punished for a crime, commits the same or another offense.

Rehabilitation - The change of an offender's behavior, mental state, and values in such a way that he ceases committing criminal acts.

Remand - To send back, as when a higher court remands a case to a lower court for a new trial, resentencing, or different handling of an issue; or when a court remands to custody one who has been free.

Right to counsel - A right guaranteed by the Sixth Amendment to the Constitution, as interpreted by the Supreme Court, permitting or necessitating representation by counsel at trial and other critical stages of the criminal process, and requiring in most instances that indigent defendants be provided with counsel for that purpose,

Scam - Organized undercover police attempts to identify and apprehend persons engaging in a variety of crimes; also, such a crime itself, particularly a confidence game.

Search and seizure - The entry of private premises or some other intrusion by government agents upon a justified expectation of privacy, and the assertion of control by such agents over a person or a thing.

Search warrant - A written order authorizing the search of a designated premises or property and the seizure of specified items as possible evidence.

Self-incrimination - Evidence presented, or testimony or other statements given, by a defendant or suspect, hurtful to himself and tending to indicate his guilt.

Sequester - To keep a jury in custodial supervision (usually in a hotel) during a trial so as to prevent contact with the public or the media; also, to separate prospective witnesses so that they cannot influence one another's testimony.

Severance - The act of separating the trials of two or more defendants or of two or more charges against a single defendant, rather than holding one trial at which the defendants or charges are tried together.

State's evidence - Testimony by a codefendant, co-conspirator, or accomplice in a crime, against the defendant and for the prosection. By turning state's evidence, a codefendant usually obtains leniency, if not complete dismissal of charges, and often requires governmental protection in a witness relocation program.

Substantive criminal law - Those sections of penal codes and other legislation that define crimes and prescribe punishments, as distinguished from procedural criminal law, which is concerned with rules governing the adjudication of the guilt or innocence of an accused.

Suspect - One who is under investigation or interrogation as a likely perpetrator of a crime but has not yet been formally charged or placed under arrest.

Vacate a judgment - To reverse a verdict or other decision of a court; to render such a verdict or decision void.

Venire - The panel of persons summoned to court from which a jury is selected.

Venireman - One summoned to serve on a jury, a juror.

Verdict - The decision handed down by the jury in a trial; to be distinguished from the findings made by a judge at a trial without jury.

Victimless crime (consensual crime) - A violation of law committed by or between two or more adults with the voluntary consent of each participant, as in adultery, sodomy, or gambling.

Voire dire - ("to see and speak") The examination of prospective jurors to determine whether they are qualified to serve on a jury.

Waiver - A relinquishment of one's rights, for example, the right to a trial by jury. Some rights may not be waived, such as the right not to suffer cruel and unusual punishment.

Warrant - An order issued by a court and authorizing an arrest or search.

Warrant, bench - A written order authorizing the arrest

of a defendant or subpoenaed witness who failed to appear on the date scheduled for his appearance in court.

Weapons charge - Violation of local, state, or federal laws governing the carrying of weapons and the licensing requirements for the purchase, sale or possession of a weapon.

White-collar crime - (See *Corporate crime*)

Witness, character - A person of good repute brought to court by the defense to testify that, based on his knowledge of the defendant and the defendant's reputation in the community, it is unlikely that he would have committed the crime charged.

Witness expert - One who qualifies as specially knowledgeable in a scientific, technical, or professional field, as a psychiatrist, examiner of documents, or geologist, and who testifies in a case on an issue in which his special training, education, and experience are useful.

Writ of error - A legal document by which appellate review is requested is requested on the ground that a lower-court decision was based on one or more errors.

APPENDIX A

STATUS OF DEATH PENALTY STATUTES, BY JURISDICTION, AS OF JANUARY 1, 1985

Note

Under State laws revised since the *Furman* decision, only specifically defined types of murder are capital offenses, Although varying somewhat from one jurisdiction to another, the types of homicde most commonly specified in these statutes are murder perpetrated during the commission of another felony; murder of a peace gaged in the performance of official duties; murder by an inmate serving a life sentence; and murder for hire.

Key

As of January 1, 1985, death penalty:

+ Was authorized
- Was not authorized

Offenses for which death penalty was authorized are listed in italics under the heading for each jurisdiction.

+ FEDERAL GOVERNMENT

Aircraft piracy resulting in death

+ ALABAMA

Murder

- ALASKA

Death penalty abolished 1957

+ ARIZONA

1st degree murder

+ ARKANSAS

Aggravated murder

+ CALIFORNIA

Murder 1st
Treason
Assault by life prisoner resulting in death
Hindering preparing for war causing death
Omitting to note defects in articles of war resulting in death
Perjury resulting in the death penalty
Train wrecking resulting in death

+ COLORADO

1st degree murder
1st degree kidnaping
Treason
Certain drug offenses (Inducing a person age 25 or under to unlawfully use or administer narcotic drugs; unlawfully use or administer narcotic drugs; unlawfully administering or dispensing a narcotic drug to a person age 25 or under; using a person age 25 or under in the unlawful transportation or production of narcotic drugs.

+ CONNECTICUT

Murder

+ DELAWARE

1st degree murder

- DISTRICT OF COLUMBIA

+ FLORIDA

Murder
Sexual battery (The sexual battery of a female child age 11 or under by a male 18 or older)

+ GEORGIA

Murder
Treason
Aircraft hijacking
Kidnaping with bodily injury
Rape when a victim dies
Armed robbery when victim dies

- HAWAII

+ IDAHO

1st degree murder
1st degree kidnaping, unless victim released unharmed

— ILLINOIS

Murder

+ INDIANA

Murder Class A felony

- IOWA

- KANSAS

+ KENTUCKY

1st degree murder
Kidnaping when victim is killed

+ LOUISIANA

1st degree murder

- MAINE

+ MARYLAND

1st degree murder

- MASSACHUSETTS

- MICHIGAN

— MINNESOTA

+ MISSISSIPPI

Murder
Treason
Aircraft piracy
Capital rape (The rape of a female child under the age of
12 by a person age 18 or older.

+ MISSOURI

Murder

+ MONTANA

Deliberate homicide
Aggravated kidnapping

+ NEBRASKA

1st degree murder

+ NEVADA
1st degree murder

+ NEW HAMPSHIRE
Murder

- NEW JERSEY

+ NEW MEXICO
1st degree murder

+ NEW YORK
Murder by life prisoner

+ NORTH CAROLINA
1st degree murder

- NORTH DAKOTA

- OHIO

+ OKLAHOMA
Murder

+ OREGON
Murder

+ PENNSYLVANIA
1st degree murder

- RHODE ISLAND

+ SOUTH CAROLINA

Murder

+ SOUTH DAKOTA

Murder
Kidnapping when gross permanent physical injury is inflicted on victim

+ TENNESSEE

1st degree murder
Rape

+ TEXAS

Murder

+ UTAH

Murder

+ VERMONT

Murder

+ VIRGINIA

Aggravated murder

+ WASHINGTON

Aggravated first degree murder

- WEST VIRGINIA

- WISCONSIN

+ WYOMING

1st degree murder
Kidnapping unless victim released unharmed

* *Death penalty retained for first-degree murder by persons who commit a second "unrelated" murder and for the first-degree murder of any law enforcement officer or prison employer in performance of duty.*

APPENDIX B

SELECTED STATE CAPITAL PUNISHMENT PROVISIONS

ARIZONA

5 Ariz. Rev. Stat.

§13-703. Sentency of death or life imprisonment without possibility of parole until the defendant has served twenty-five calendar years:

A. A person guilty of first degree murder as defined in §13-1105 shall suffer death or imprisonment in the custody of the department of corrections for life, without possibility of parole until the completion of the service of twenty-five calendar years, as determined and in accordance with the procedures provided in subsections B through G of this section.

B. When a defendant is found guilty of or pleads guilty to first degree murder as defined in §13-1105, the judge who presided at the trial or before whom the guilty plea was entered, or any other judge to the event of the death, resignation, incapacity or disqualification of the judge who presided at trial or before whom the guilty plea was entered, shall conduct a separate sentencing hearing to determine the existence or nonexistence of the circumstances included in subsection F and G of this section, for the purpose of determining the sentence to be imposed. The hearing shall be conducted before the court alone.

C. In the sentencing hearing the court shall disclose to the defendant or defendant's counsel all material contained in any presentence report, if one has been prepared, except such material as the court determines is required to be withheld for the protection of human life. Any presentence information withheld from the defendant shall not be subsection F or G of this section. Any information relevant to any mitigating circumstances included in subsection G of this section may be presented by either the prosecution or the defendant, regardless of its admissibility under the rules governing admission of evidence at criminal trials, but the admissibility of information relevant to any of the aggravating circumstances set forth in subsection F of this section shall be governed by the rules governing the admission of evidence at criminal trials. Evidence admitted at the trial, relating to such aggravating or mitigating circumstances, shall be considered without reintroducing it at the sentencing proceeding. The prosecution and the defendant shall be permitted to rebut any information received at the hearing and shall be given fair opportunity to present argument as to the adequacy of the information to establish the existence of any of the circumstances included in subsections F and G of this section. The burden of establishing the existence of any of the circumstances set forth in subsection F of this section is on the prosecution. The burden of establishing the existence of the circumstances included in subsection G of this section is on the defendant.

D. The court shall return a special verdict setting forth its findings as to the existence or nonexistence of each of the circumstances set forth in subsection F of this section and as to the existence of any of the circumstances included in subsection G of this section.

E. In determining whether to impose a sentence of death or life imprisonment without possibility of parole until the defendant has served twenty-five calendar years, the court shall take into account the aggravating and mitigating circumstances included in subsections F and G of this section and shall impose a sentence of death if the court finds one ore more of the aggravating circumstances enumerated in subsection F of this section and that there are no mitigating circumstances sufficiently substantial to call for leniency.

F. Aggravating circumstances to be considered shall be the following:

1. The defendant has been convicted of another offense in the United States for which under Arizona law a sentence of life imprisonment or death was imposable.

2. The defendant was previously convicted of a felony in the United States involving the use or threat of violence on another person.

3. In the commission of the offense the defendant knowingly created a grave risk of death to another person or persons in addition to the victim of the offense.

4. The defendant procured the commission of the offense by payment, or promise of payment, of anything of pecuniary value.

5. The defendant committed the offense as consideration for the receipt, or in expectation of the receipt, of anything of pecuniary value.

6. The defendant committed the offense in an especially heinous, cruel or depraved manner.

7. The defendant committed the offense while in the custody of the department of corrections, a law enforcement agency or county or city jail.

8. The defendant has been convicted of one or more other homicides, as defined in §13-1101, which were committed during the commission of the offense.

G. Mitigating circumstances shall be any factors proffered by the defendant or the state which are relevant in determining whether to impose a sentence less than death, including any aspect of the defendant's character, propensities or record and any of the circumstances of the offense, including but not limited to the following:

1. The defendant's capacity to appreciate the wrongfulness of his conduct or to conform his conduct to the requirements of law was significantly impaired, but not so impaired as to constitute a defense to prosecution.

2. The defendant was under unusual and substantial duress, although not such as to constitute a defense to prosecution.

3. The defendant was legally accountable for the conduct of another under the provisions of §13-303, but his participation was relatively minor, although not so minor as to constitute a defense to prosecution.

4. The defendant could not reasonably have foreseen that his conduct in the course of the commission of the offense for which the defendant was convicted

106

would cause, or would create a grave risk of causing, death to another person.

5. The defendant's age.

ARKANSAS

(4 Ark. Stat.)

41-1310-41-1350

A person convicted of a capital offense shall be punished by death by electrocution or by life imprisonment without parole pursuant to Chapter 13.

41-1352

The punishment by death is hereafter to be administered by a continuous intravenous injection of a lethal quantity of an ultra-short-acting barbituate in combination with a chemical paralytic agent until the defendant's death is pronounced according to accepted standards of medical practice. The Director of Correction shall determine the substances to be uniformly administered and the procedures to be used in any execution.

41-1354. Election of manner of execution by defendants sentenced to death by electrocution.

Any defendant currently sentenced to death by electrocution or any defendant sentenced to death by electrocution prior to the effective date [July 4, 1983] of this Act may elect to be executed by lethal injection pursuant to the provisions of this Act [§§41-1352—41-1357]. Such election must be exercised in writing one [1] week prior to the date of execution or be deemed waived. [Acts 1983, No. 774, §3, p. 1804.]

41-1355. References to execution by electrocution to mean execution by lethal injection.

All references in the laws of the State of Arkansas relating to execution by electrocution shall, insofar as such provisions are applicable, apply to, and mean, execution by lethal injection, except as to capital offenses already committed. [Acts 1983, No. 774, §4, p. 1804.]

41-1356. Execution by electrocution in event that death by lethal injection held unconstitutional.

If the execution of the sentence of death as provided in section one (1) [§41-1352] of this Act is held unconstitutional by an appellate court of competent jurisdiction, then the sentence of death shall be carried out by electrocution in a manner determined by the director of the department of correction. [Acts 1983, No. 774, §5, p. 1804.]

41-1357. Death by electrocution not declared cruel and unusual punishment

Nothing in this Act [§§41-1352—41-1357] is to be construed as a declaration by the Arkansas General Assembly that death by electrocution constitutes cruel and unusual punishment in violation of the constitutions of the United States or the State of Arkansas. [Acts 1983, No. 774, §6, p. 1804.]

41-1358. Procedures following remand of capital case after vacation of death sentence—Retroactive application.

Notwithstanding subsection (3) of Section 1301 of Act 280 of 1975, [Ark. Stat. Ann. §41-1301(3)], which requires that the same jury sit in the sentencing phase of a capital murder trial, the following shall apply:

(a) Upon any appeal by the defendant where the sentence is of death, the appellate court, if it finds prejudicial error in the sentencing proceeding only, may set aside the sentence of death and remand the case to the trial court in the jurisdiction in which the defendant was originally sentenced. No error in the sentencing proceeding shall result in the reversal of the conviction for a capital felony.

When a capital case is remanded after vacation of a death sentence, the prosecutor may:

(1) Move the trial court to impose a sentence of life without parole and the trial court may impose such sentence without a hearing;

(2) Move the trial court to impanel a new sentencing jury.

(b) If the prosecutor elects (a)(2), above, the trial court shall impanel a new jury for the purpose of conducting new sentencing proceedings;

(c) Resentencing proceedings shall be governed by the provisions of §§1301(4), 1302, 1303, and 1304 of Act 280 of 1975, as amended;

(d) All exhibits and a transcript of all testimony and other evidence properly admitted in the prior trial and sentencing shall be admissible in the new sentencing proceeding; additional relevant evidence may be admitted including testimony of witnesses who testified at the previous trial;

(e) The provisions of this Act [this section] are procedural; they shall apply retroactively to any defendant sentenced to death after January 1, 1974.

(f) This Act shall not be construed to amend the provisions of Section 1303(3) [Section 1301(3)][§41-1301] of Act 280 of 1975 requiring the same jury to sit in both the guilt and sentencing phases of the original trial. [Acts 1983, No. 546, §1, p. 1804.]

CALIFORNIA

47 Annotated Cal. Code

§190.2. Death penalty or life imprisonment without parole; special circumstances

(a) The penalty for a defendant found guilty of murder in the first degree shall be death or confinement in state prison for a term of life without the possibility of parole in any case in which one or more of the following special circumstances has been charged and specially found under Section 190.4, to be true:

(1) The murder was intentional and carried out for financial gain.

(2) The defendant was previously convicted of murder in the first degree or

108

second degree. For the purpose of this paragraph an offense committed in another jurisdiction which if committed in California would be punishable as first or second degree murder shall be deemed murder in the first or second degree.

(3) The defendant has in this proceeding been convicted of more than one offense of murder in the first or second degree.

(4) The murder was committed by means of a destructive device, bomb, or explosive planted, hidden or concealed in any place, area, dwelling, building or structure, and the defendant knew or reasonably should have known that his act or acts would create a great risk of death to a human being or human beings.

(5) The murder was committed for the purpose of avoiding or preventing a lawful arrest or to perfect, or attempt to perfect an escape from lawful custody.

(6) The murder was committed by means of a destructive device, bomb, or explosive that the defendant mailed or delivered, attempted to mail or deliver, or cause to be mailed or delivered and the defendant knew or reasonably should have known that his act or acts would create a great risk of death to a human being or human beings.

(7) The victim was a peace officer as defined in Section 830.1, 830.2, 830.3, 830.31, 830.35, 830.36, 830.4, 830.5, 830.5a, 830.6, 830.10, 830.11 or 830.12, who, while engaged in the course of the performance of his duties was intentionally killed, and such defendant knew or reasonably should have known that such victim was a peace officer engaged in the performance of his duties; or the victim was a peace officer as defined in the above enumerated sections of the Penal Code, or a former peace officer under any of such sections, and was intentionally killed in retaliation for the performance of his official duties.

(8). The victim was a federal law enforcement officer or agent, who, while engaged in the course of the performance of his duties was intentionally killed, and such defendant knew or reasonably should have known that such victim was a federal law enforcement officer or agent, engaged in the performance of his duties; or the victim was a federal law enforcement officer or agent, and was intentionally killed in retaliation for the performance of his official duties.

(9) The victim was a fireman as defined in Section 245.1, who while engaged in the course of the performance of his duties was intentionally killed, and such defendant knew or reasonably should have known that such victim was a fireman engaged in the performance of his duties.

(10) The victim was a witness to a crime who was intentionally killed for the purpose of preventing his testimony in any criminal proceeding, and the killing was not committed during the commission, or attempted commission or the crime to which he was a witness; or the victim was a witness to a crime and was intentionally killed in retaliation for his testimony in any criminal proceeding.

(11) The victim was a prosecutor or assistant prosecutor or a former prosecutor or assistant prosecutor of any local or state prosecutor's office in this state or any other state, or a federal prosecutor's office and the murder was carried out in retaliation for or to prevent the performance of the victim's official duties.

(12) The victim was a judge or former judge of any court of record in the

local, state or federal system in the State of California or in any other state of the United States and the murder was carried out in retaliation for or to prevent the performance of the victim's official duties.

(13) The victim was an elected or appointed official or former official of the Federal Government, a local or State government of California, or of any local or state government of any other state in the United States and the killing was intentionally carried out in retaliation for or to prevent the performance of the victim's official duties.

(14) The murder was especially heinous, atrocious, or cruel, manifesting exceptional depravity, as utilized in this section, the phrase especially heinous, atrocious or cruel manifesting exceptional depravity means a conscienceless, or pitiful crime which is unnecessarily torturous to the victim.

(15) The defendant intentionally killed the victim while lying in wait.

(16) The victim was intentionally killed because of his race, color, religion, nationality or country of origin.

(17) The murder was committed while the defendant was engaged in or was an accomplice in the commission of, attempted commission of, or the immediate flight after committing or attempting to commit the following felonies:

(i) Robbery in violation of Section 211.

(ii) Kidnapping in violation of Sections 207 and 209.

(iii) Rape in violation of Section 261.

(iv) Sodomy in violation of Section 286.

(v) The performance of a lewd or lascivious act upon person of a child under the age of 14 in violation of Section 288.

(vi) Oral copulation in violation of Section 288a.

(vii) Burglary in the first or second degree in violation of Section 460.

(viii) Arson in violation of Section 447.

(ix) Train wrecking in violation of Section 219.

(18) The murder was intentional and involved the infliction of torture. For the purpose of this section torture requires proof of the infliction of extreme physical pain no matter how long its duration.

(19) The defendant intentionally killed the victim by the administration of poison.

(b) Every person whether or not the actual killer found guilty of intentionally aiding, abetting, counseling, commanding, inducing, soliciting, requesting, or assisting any actor in the commission of murder in the first degree shall suffer death or confinement in state prison for a term of life without the possibility of parole, in any case in which one or more of the special circumstances enumerated in paragraphs (1), (3), (4), (5), (6), (7), (8), (9), (10), (11), (12), (13), (14), (15), (16), (17), (18), or (19) of subdivision (a) of this section has been charged and specially found under Section 190.4 to be true.

The penalty shall be determined as provided in Sections 190.1, 190.2, 190.3, 190.4, and 190.5.

§190.3. Death penalty or life imprisonment; determination by trier; evidence of aggravating and mitigating circumstances; factors

If the defendant has been found guilty of murder in the first degree, and a special circumstance has been charged and found to be true, or if the defendant may be subject to the death penalty after having been found guilty of violating subdivision (a) of Section 1672 of the Military and Veterans Code or Sections 37, 128, 219, or 4500 of this code, the trier of fact shall determine whether the penalty shall be death or confinement in state prison for a term of life without the possibility of parole. In the proceedings on the question of penalty, evidence may be presented by both the people and the defendant as to any matter relevant to aggravation, mitigation, and sentence including, but not limited to, the nature and circumstances of the present offense, any prior felony conviction or convictions whether or not such conviction or convictions involved a crime of violence, the presence or absence of other criminal activity by the defendant which involved the use or attempted use of force or violence or which involved the express or implied threat to use force or violence, and the defendant's character, background, history, mental condition and physical condition.

However, no evidence shall be admitted regarding other criminal activity by the defendant which did not involve the use or attempted use of force or violence or which did not involve the express or implied threat to use force or violence. As used in this section, criminal activity does not require a conviction.

However, in no event shall evidence of prior criminal activity be admitted for an offense for which the defendant was prosecuted and acquitted. The restriction on the use of this evidence is intended to apply only to proceedings pursuant to this section and is not intended to affect statutory or decisional law allowing such evidence to be used in any other proceedings.

Except for evidence in proof of the offense or special circumstances which subject a defendant to the death penalty, no evidence may be presented by the prosecution in aggravation unless notice of the evidence to be introduced has been given to the defendant within a reasonable period of time as determined by the court, prior to trial. Evidence may be introduced without such notice in rebuttal to evidence introduced by the defendant in mitigation.

The trier of fact shall be instructed that a sentence of confinement to state prison for a term of life without the possibility of parole may in future after sentence is imposed, be commuted or modified to a sentence that includes the possibility of parole by the Governor of the State of California.

In determining the penalty, the trier fact shall take into account any of the following factors if relevant:

(a) The circumstances of the crime of which the defendant was convicted in the present proceeding and the existence of any special circumstances found to be true pursuant to Section 190.1.

(b) The presence or absence of criminal activity by the defendant which involved the use or attempted use of force or violence or the express or implied threat to use force or violence.

(c) The presence or absence of any prior felony conviction.

111

(d) Whether or not the offense was committed while the defendant was under the influence of extreme mental or emotional disturbance.

(e) Whether or not the victim was a participant in the homicidal conduct or consented to the homicidal act.

(f) Whether or not the offense was committed under circumstances which the defendant reasonable believed to be a moral justification or extenuation for his conduct.

(g) Whether or not defendant acted under extreme duress or under the substantial domination of another person.

(h) Whether or not at the time of the offense the capacity of the defendant to appreciate the criminality of his conduct or to conform his conduct to the requirements of law was impaired as a result of mental disease or defect, or the affects of intoxication.

(i) The age of the defendant at the time of the crime.

(j) Whether or not the defendant was an accomplice to the offense and his participation in the commission of the offense was relatively minor.

(k) Any other circumstance which extenuates the gravity of the crime even though it is not a legal excuse for the crime.

After having heard and received all of the evidence, and after having heard and considered the arguments of counsel, the trier of fact shall consider, take into account and be guided by the aggravating and mitigating circumstances referred to in this section, and shall impose a sentence of death if the trier of fact concludes that the aggravating circumstances outweigh the mitigating circumstances. If the trier of fact determines that the mitigating circumstances outweigh the aggravating circumstances the trier of fact shall impose a sentence of confinement in state prison for a term of life without the possibility of parole.

§190.5. Death penalty; exclusion of persons under 18; proof

Notwithstanding any other provision of law, the death penalty shall not be imposed upon any person who is under the age of 18 at the time of the commission of the crime. The burden of proof as to the age of such person shall be upon the defendant.

§190.6. Legislature finding; limitations

The Legislature finds that the imposition of sentence in all capital cases should be expeditiously carried out.

Therefore, in all cases in which a sentence of death has been imposed, the appeal to the State Supreme Court must be decided and an opinion reaching the merits must be filed within 150 days of certification of the entire record by the sentencing court. In any case in which this time requirement is not met, the Chief Justice of the Supreme Court shall state on the record the extraordinary and compelling circumstances causing the delay and the facts supporting these circumstances. A failure to comply with the time requirements of this section shall not be grounds for precluding the ultimate imposition of the death penalty.

DEATH PENALTY-EXECUTION

16-11-402. Appliances - sentence executed by executive director.

The executive director of the department of corrections, at the expense of the state of Colorado, shall provide a suitable and efficient room or place, enclosed from public view, within the walls of the correctional facilities at Canon City and therein construct and at all times have in preparation all necessary appliances requisite for carrying into execution the death penalty by means of the administration of lethal gas. The punishment of death in each case of death sentence pronounced in this state shall be inflicted by the executive director or his designee in the room or place and with the appliances provided for inflicting the punishment of death by the administration of lethal gas.

16-11-403. Week of execution - warrant.

When a person is convicted of a class 1 felony, the punishment for which is death, and the convicted person is sentenced to suffer the penalty of death, the judge passing such sentence shall appoint and designate in the warrant of conviction a week of time within which the sentence must be executed; the end of such week so appointed shall not be less than ninety days nor more than one hundred twenty days from the day of passing the sentence. Said warrant shall be directed to the executive director of the department of corrections or his designee commanding said executive director or his designee to execute the sentence imposed upon some day within the week of time designated in the warrant and shall be delivered to the sheriff of the county in which such conviction is had, who, within three days thereafter, shall proceed to the correctional facilities at Canon City and deliver the convicted person, together with the warrant, to said executive director or his designee, who shall keep the convict in confinement until infliction of the death penalty. No person shall be allowed access to said convict, except his attendants, counsel, and physician, a spiritual adviser of his own selection, and members of his family, and then only in accordance with prison regulations.

16-11-404. Execution - witnesses.

The particular day and hour of the execution of said sentence within the week specified in said warrant shall be fixed by the executive director of the department of corrections or his designee but shall not be made public by him, and he shall be present thereat or shall appoint some other representative among the officials or officers of the correctional facilities at Canon City to be present in his place and stead. There shall also be present a physician and such guards, attendants, and other persons as the executive director or his designee in his discretion deems desirable, not to exceed fifteen persons. The executive director or his designee shall notify the governor of the day and hour for the execution as soon as it has been fixed.

113

16-11-405. Record and certificate of execution.

The executive director of the department of corrections or his designee shall keep a book of record, to be known as record of executions, in which shall be entered the reports specified in this section. Immediately after the execution, a postmortem examination of the body of the convict shall be made by the attending physician, who shall enter in said book of record the nature and extent of the examination and sign and certify to the same. The executive director or his designee shall also immediately make and enter in said book a report, setting forth the time of such execution and that the convict (naming him) was then

CONNECTICUT

27A Conn. Gen. Stat. Annotated

§ 53a-35a. Imprisonment for any felony committed on or after July 1, 1981: Definite sentences; terms authorized

For any felony committed on or after July 1, 1981, the sentence of imprisonment shall be a definite sentence and the term shall be fixed by the court as follows: (1) For a capital felony, a term of life unless a sentence of death is imposed in accordance with section 53a-46a;

§ 53a-46a. Hearing on imposition of death penalty. Aggravating and mitigating factors

(a) A person shall be subjected to the penalty of death for a capital felony only if a hearing is held in accordance with the provisions of this section.

(b) For the purpose of determining the sentence to be imposed when a defendant is convicted of or pleads guilty to a capital felony, the judge or judges who presided at the trial or before whom the guilty plea was entered shall conduct a separate hearing to determine the existence of any mitigating factor concerning the defendant's character, background and history, or the nature and circumstances of the crime, including any mitigating factor set forth in subsection (f), and any aggravating factor set forth in subsection (g). Such hearing shall not be held if the state stipulates that none of the aggravating factors set forth in subsection (g) of this section exists or that one or more mitigating factors exists. Such hearing shall be conducted (1) before the jury which determined the defendant's guilt, or (2) before a jury impaneled for the purpose of such hearing if (A) the defendant was convicted upon a plea of guilty; (B) the defendant was convicted after a trial before three judges as provided in subsection (b) of section 53a-45; or (C) if the jury which determined the defendant's guilt has been discharged by the court for good cause or, (3) before the court, on motion of the defendant and with the approval of the court and the consent of the state.

(c) In such hearing the court shall disclose to the defendant or his counsel all material contained in any presentence report which may have been prepared. No presentence information withheld from the defendant shall be considered in

114

determining the existence of any mitigating or aggravating factor. Any information relevant to any mitigating factor may be presented by either the state or the defendant, regardless of its admissibility under the rules governing admission of evidence in trials of criminal matters, but the admissibility of information relevant to any of the aggravating factors set forth in subsection (g) shall be governed by the rules governing the admission of evidence in such trials. The state and the defendant shall be permitted to rebut any information received at the hearing and shall be given fair opportunity to present argument as to the adequacy of the information to establish the existence of any mitigating or aggravating factor. The burden of establishing any of the factors set forth in subsection (g) shall be on the state. The burden of establishing any mitigating factor shall be on the defendant.

(d) The jury or, if there is no jury, the court shall return a special verdict setting forth its findings as to the existence of any aggravating or mitigating factor.

(e) If the jury or, if there is no jury, the court finds that one or more of the factors set forth in subsection (g) exists and that no mitigating factor exists, the court shall sentence the defendant to death. If the jury or, if there is no jury, the court finds that none of the factors set forth in subsection (g) exists or that one or more mitigating factors exist, the court shall impose a sentence in accordance with subdivision (1) of section 53a-35a.

(f) The court shall not impose the sentence of death on the defendant if the jury or, if there is no jury, the court finds by a special verdict, as provided in subsection (d), that any mitigating factor exists. The mitigating factors to be considered concerning the defendant shall include, but are not limited to, the following: That at the time of the offense (1) he was under the age of eighteen or (2) his mental capacity was significantly impaired or his ability to conform his conduct to the requirements of law was significantly impaired but not so impaired in either case as to constitute a defense to prosecution or (3) he was under unusual and substantial duress, although not such duress as to constitute a defense to prosecution or (4) he was criminally liable under sections 53a-8, 53a-9 and 53a-10 for the offense, which was committed by another, but his participation in such offense was relatively minor, although not so minor as to constitute a defense to prosecution or (5) he could not reasonably have foreseen that his conduct in the course of commission of the offense of which he was convicted would cause, or would create a grave risk of causing, death to another person.

(g) If no mitigating factor is present, the court shall impose the sentence of death on the defendant if the jury or, if there is no jury, the court finds by a special verdict as provided in subsection (d) that (1) the defendant committed the offense during the commission or attempted commission of, or during the immediate flight from the commission or attempted commission of, a felony and he had previously been convicted of the same felony; or (2) the defendant committed the offense after having been convicted of two or more state offenses or two or more federal offenses or of one or more state offenses and one or more federal offenses for each of which a penalty of more than one year imprisonment may be imposed, which offenses were committed on different occasions and which involved the infliction of serious bodily injury upon another person; or (3) the defendant committed the offense and in such commission knowingly created a grave risk of death to another person in addition to the victim of the offense; or (4) the defendant committed the offense in an especially heinous, cruel or depraved manner; or (5) the defendant procured the commission of the offense by payment, or promise of payment, of anything of pecuniary value; or (6) the defendant committed the offense as consideration for the receipt, or in expectation of the receipt, of anything of pecuniary value.

GEORGIA

15 Ga. Code

ARTICLE 2
DEATH PENALTY GENERALLY

17-10-30. Procedure for imposition of death penalty generally.

(a) The death penalty may be imposed for the offenses of aircraft hijacking or treason in any case.

(b) In all cases of other offenses for which the death penalty may be authorized, the judge shall consider, or he shall include in his instructions to the jury for it to consider, any mitigating circumstances or aggravating circumstances, otherwise authorized by law and any of the following statutory aggravating circumstances which may be supported by the evidence:

(1) The offense of murder, rape, armed robbery, or kidnapping was committed by a person with a prior record of conviction for a capital felony;

(2). The offense of murder, rape, armed robbery, or kidnapping was committed while the offender was engaged in the commission of another capital felony or aggravated battery, or the offense of murder was committed while the offender was engaged in the commission of burglary or arson in the first degree;

(3) The offender, by his act of murder, armed robbery, or kidnapping, knowingly created a great risk of death to more than one person in a public place by means of a weapon or device which would normally be hazardous to the lives of more than one person;

(4) The offender committed the offense of murder for himself or another, for the purpose of receiving money or any other thing of monetary value;

(5) The murder of a judicial officer, former judicial officer, district attorney or solicitor, or former district attorney or solicitor was committed during or because of the exercise of his official duties;

(6) The offender caused or directed another to commit murder or committed murder as an agent or employee of another person;

(7) The offense of murder, rape, armed robbery, or kidnapping was outrageously or wantonly vile, horrible, or inhuman in that it involved torture, depravity of mind, or an aggravated battery to the victim;

116

(8) The offense of murder was committed against any peace officer, corrections employee, or fireman while engaged in the performance of his official duties;

(9) The offense of murder was committed by a person in, or who has escaped from, the lawful custody of a peace officer or place of lawful confinement; or

(10) The murder was committed for the purpose of avoiding, interfering with, or preventing a lawful arrest or custody in a place of lawful confinement, of himself or another.

(c) The statutory instructions as determined by the trial judge to be warranted by the evidence shall be given in charge and in writing to the jury for its deliberation. The jury, of its verdict is a recommendation of death, shall designate in writing, signed by the foreman of the jury, the aggravating circumstance or circumstances which it found beyond a reasonable doubt. In nonjury cases the judge shall make such designation. Except in cases of treason or aircraft hijacking, unless at least one of the statutory aggravating circumstances enumerated in subsection (b) of this Code section is so found, the death penalty shall not be imposed. (Code 1933, §27-2534.1, enacted by Ga. L. 1973, p. 159, §3.)

17-10-31. Requirement of jury finding of aggravating circumstance and recommendation that death penalty be imposed prior to imposition of death sentence.

Where, upon a trial by jury, a person is convicted of an offense which may be punishable by death, a sentence of death shall not be imposed unless the jury verdict includes a finding of at least one statutory aggravating circumstance and a recommendation that such sentence be imposed. Where a statutory aggravating circumstance is found and a recommendation of death is made, the court shall sentence the defendant to death. Where a sentence of death is not recommended by the jury, the court shall sentence the defendant to imprisonment as provided by law. Unless the jury trying the case makes a finding of at least one statutory aggravating circumstance and recommends the death sentence in its verdict, the court shall not sentence the defendant to death, provided that no such finding of statutory aggravating circumstance shall be necessary in offenses of treason or aircraft hijacking. This Code section shall not affect a sentence when the case is tried without a jury or when the judge accepts a plea of guilty. (Code 1933, §26-3102, enacted by Ga. L. 1968, p. 1249, §1; Ga. L. 1969, p. 809, §1; Ga. L. 1973, p. 159, §7.)

17-10-32. Sentencing of person indicted for capital offense to life imprisonment or other punishment upon entry of plea of guilty.

Any person who has been indicted for an offense punishable by death may enter a plea of guilty at any time after his indictment, and the judge of the superior court having jurisdiction may, in his discretion, sentence the person to life imprisonment or to any other punishment authorized by law for the offense named in the indictment; provided, however, that the judge must find one of the statutory aggravating circumstances provided in Code Section 17-10-30 before imposing the death penalty, except in cases of treason or aircraft hijacking. (Ga. L. 1956, p. 737, §1; Ga. L. 1973, p. 159, §8.)

ILLINOIS

28 Ill. Anno. St.

§9-1. Murder—Death penalties—Exceptions—Separate Hearings—Proof— Findings—Appellate procedures—Reversals.

(a) A person who kills an individual without lawful justification commits murder if, in performing the acts which cause (1) He either intends to kill or do great bodily harm to that individual or another, or knows that such acts will cause death to that individual or another; or

(2) He knows that such acts create a strong probability of death or great bodily harm to that individual or another; or

(3) He is attempting or committing a forcible felony other than voluntary manslaughter.

(b) **Aggravating Factors.** A defendant who at the time of the commission of the offense has attained the age of 18 or more and who has been found guilty of murder may be sentenced to death if:

1 The murdered individual was a peace officer or fireman killed in the course of performing his official duties and the defendant knew or should have known that the murdered individual was a peace officer or fireman; or

2 the murdered individual was an employee of an institution or facility of the Department of Corrections, or any similar local correctional agency, killed in the course of performing his official duties, or the murdered individual was an inmate at such institution or facility and was killed on the grounds thereof, or the murdered individual was otherwise present in such institution or facility with the knowledge and approval of the chief administrative officer thereof; or

3 the defendant has been convicted of murdering two or more individuals under subsection (a) of this Section or under any law of the United States or of any state which is substantially similar to subsection (a) of this Section regardless of whether the deaths occurred as the result of the same act or of several related or unrelated acts so long as the deaths were the result of either an intent to kill more than one person or of separate premeditated acts; or

4 the murder individual was killed as a result of the hijacking of an airplane, train, ship, bus or other public conveyance; or

5 the defendant committed the murder pursuant to a contract, agreement or understanding by which he was to receive money or anything of value in return for committing the murder or procured another to commit the murder for money or anything of value; or

6 the murdered individual was killed in the course of another felony if:

(a) the murdered individual:

(i) was actually killed by the defendant, or

(ii) received physical injuries personally inflicted by the defendant substantially contemporaneously with physical injuries caused by one or more

118

persons for whose conduct the defendant is legally accountable under Section 5-2 of this Code, and the physical injuries inflicted by either the defendant or the other person or persons for whose conduct he is legally accountable caused the death of the murdered individual; and

(b) in performing the acts which caused the death of the murdered individual or which resulted in physical injuries personally inflicted by the defendant on the murdered individual under the circumstances of subdivision (ii) of subparagraph (a) of paragraph (6) of subsection (b) of this Section, the defendant acted with the intent to kill the murdered individual or with the knowledge that his acts created a strong probability of death or great bodily harm to the murdered individual or another; and

(c) the other felony was one of the following: armed robbery, robbery, aggravated criminal sexual assault, aggravated kidnapping, forcible detention, arson, aggravated arson, burglarly, home invasion, or the attempt to commit any of the felonies listed in this subsection (c); or

7. the murdered individual was under 12 years of age and the death resulted from exceptionally brutal or heinous behavior indicative of wanton cruelty; or

8. the defendant committed the murder with intent to prevent the murdered individual from testifying in any criminal prosecution or giving material assistance to the State in any investigation or prosecution, either against the defendant or another; or the defendant committed the murder because the murdered individual was a witness in any prosecution or gave material assistance to the State in any investigation or prosecution, either against the defendant or another.

(c) Consideration of factors in Aggravation and Mitigation. The court shall consider, or shall instruct the jury to consider any aggravating and any mitigating factors which are relevant to the imposition of the death penalty. Aggravating factors may include but need not be limited to those factors set forth in subsection (b). Mitigating factors may include but need not be limited to the following:

1. the defendant has no significant history of prior criminal activity;

2. the murder was committed while the defendant was under the influence of extreme mental or emotional disturbance, although not such as to constitute a defense to prosecution;

3. the murdered individual was a participant in the defendant's homicidal conduct or consented to the homicidal act;

4. the defendant acted under the compulsion of threat or menace of the imminent infliction of death or great bodily harm;

5. the defendant was not personally present during commission of the act or acts causing death.

(d) Separate sentencing hearing. Where requested by the State, the court shall conduct a separate sentencing proceeding to determine the existence of factors set forth in subsection (h) and to consider any aggravating or mitigating factors as indicated in subsection (c). The proceedings shall be conducted:

1. before the jury that determined the defendant's guilt; or

2. before a jury impanelled for the purpose of the proceeding if:

A. the defendant was convicted upon a plea of guilty; or

B. the defendant was convicted after a trial before the court sitting without a jury; or

C. the court for good cause shown discharges the jury that determined the defendant's guilt; or

3. before the court alone if the defendant waives a jury for the separate proceeding.

(e) **Evidence and Argument.** During the proceeding any information relevant to any of the factors set forth in subsection (b) may be presented by either the State or the defendant under the rules governing the admission of evidence at criminal trials. Any information relevant to any additional aggravating factors or any mitigating factors indicated in subsection (c) may be presented by the State or defendant regardless of its admissibility under the rules governing the admission of evidence at criminal trials. The State and the defendant shall be given fair opportunity to rebut any information received at the hearing.

(f) **Proof.** The burden of proof of establishing the existence of any of the factors set forth in subsection (b) is on the State and shall not be satisfied unless established beyond a reasonable doubt.

(g) **Procedure—Jury.** If at the separate sentencing proceeding the jury finds that none of the factors set forth in subsection (b) exists, the court shall sentence the defendant to a term of imprisonment under Chapter V of the Unified Code of Corrections.[1] If there is a unanimous finding by the jury that one or more of the factors set forth in subsection (b) exist, the jury shall consider aggravating and mitigating factors as instructed by the court and shall determine whether the sentence of death shall be imposed. If the jury determines unanimously that there are no mitigating factors sufficient to preclude the imposition of the death sentence, the court shall sentence the defendant to death.

Unless the jury unanimously finds that there are no mitigating factors sufficient to preclude the imposition of the death sentence the court shall sentence the defendant to a term of imprisonment under Chapter V of the Unified Code of Corrections.

(h) **Procedure—No Jury.** In a proceeding before the court alone, if the court finds that none of the factors found in subsection (b) exists, the court shall

KENTUCKY

16 Anno. Ky. Rev. Stat.

507.020. Murder.—(1) A person is guilty of murder when:

(a) With intent to cause the death of another person, he causes the death of such person or of a third person; except that in any prosecution a person shall not be guilty under this subsection if he acted under the influence of extreme emotional disturbance for which there was a reasonable explanation or excuse, the reasonableness of which is to be determined from the viewpoint of a person in the defendant's situation under the circumstances as the defendant believed them to be. However, nothing contained in this section shall constitute a defense to a prosecution for or preclude a conviction of manslaughter in the first degree or any other crime;

(b) Including, but not limited to, the operation of a motor vehicle under curcumstances manifesting extreme indifference to human life, he wantonly engages in conduct which creates a grave risk of death to another person and thereby causes the death of another person.

(2) Murder is a capital offense. (Enact. Acts 1974, ch. 406, §61; 1976, ch. 183, §1; 1976 (Ex. Sess.), ch. 15, §1, effective December 22, 1976; 1984, ch. 165, §26, effective July 13, 1984.)

35-50-2-9. Death sentences. —

(a) The state may seek a death sentence for murder by alleging, on a page separate from the rest of the charging instrument, the existence of at least one of the aggravating circumstances listed in subsection (b). In the sentencing hearing after a person is convicted of murder, the state must prove beyond a reasonable doubt the existence of at least one of the aggravating circumstances alleged.

(b) The aggravating circumstances are as follows:

(1) The defendant committed the murder by intentionally killing the victim while committing or attempting to commit arson, burglary, child molesting, criminal deviate conduct, kidnapping, rape, or robbery.

(2) The defendant committed the murder by the unlawful detonation of an explosive with intent to injure person or damage property.

(3) The defendant committed the murder by lying in wait.

(4) The defendant who committed the murder was hired to kill.

(5) The defendant committed the murder by hiring another person to kill.

(6) The victim of the murder was a corrections employee, fireman, judge, or law enforcement officer, and either (i) the victim was acting in the course of duty or (ii) the murder was motivated by an act the victim performed while acting in the course of duty.

(7) The defendant has been convicted of another murder.

(8) The defendant has committed another murder, at any time, regardless of whether he has been convicted of that other murder.

(9) The defendant was under a sentence of life imprisonment at the time of the murder.

(10) The defendant was serving a term of imprisonment and on the date of the murder the defendant had twenty [20] or more years remaining to be served before his earliest possible release date as defined by IC 35-38.

(c) The mitigating circumstances that may be considered under the section are as follows:

(1) The defendant has no significant history of prior criminal conduct.

(2) The defendant was under the influence of extreme mental or emotional disturbance when he committed the murder.

(3) The victim was a participant in, or consented to, the defendant's conduct.

(4) The defendant was an accomplice in a murder committed by another person, and the defendant's participation was relatively minor.

121

(5) The defendant acted under the substantial domination of another person.

(6) The defendant's capacity to appreciate the criminality of his conduct or to conform his conduct to the requirements of law was substantially impaired as a result of mental disease or defect or of intoxication.

(7) Any other circumstances appropriate for consideration.

(d) If the defendant was convicted of murder in a jury trial, the jury shall reconvene for the sentencing hearing; if the trial was to the court, or the judgment was entered on a guilty plea, the court alone shall conduct the sentencing hearing. The jury or the court may consider all the evidence intorduced at the trial stage of the proceedings, together with new evidence presented at the sentencing hearing. The defendant may present any additional evidence relevant to:

(1) The aggravating circumstances alleged; or

(2) Any of the mitigating circumstances listed in subsection (c).

(e) If the hearing is by jury, the jury shall recommend to the court whether the death penalty should be imposed. The jury may recommend the death penalty only if it finds:

(1) That the state has proved beyond a reasonable doubt that at least one of the aggravating circumstances exists; and

(2) That any mitigating circumstances that exist are outweighed by the aggravating circumstance or circumstances.

The court shall make the final determination of the sentence, after considering the jury's recommendation, and the sentence shall be based on the same standards that the jury was required to consider. The court is not bound by the jury's recommendation.

(f) If a jury is unable to agree on a sentence recommendation after reasonable deliberations, the court shall discharge the jury and proceed as if the hearing had been to the court alone.

(g) If the hearing is to the court alone, the court shall sentence the defendant to death only if it finds:

(1) That the state has proved beyond a reasonable doubt that at least one of the aggravating circumstances exists; and

(2) That any mitigating circumstances that exist are outweighed by the aggravating circumstance or circumstances.

(h) A death sentence is subject to automatic review by the supreme court. The review, which shall be heard under rules adopted by the supreme court, shall be given priority over all other cases. The death sentence may not be executed until the supreme court has completed its review. [IC 35-50-2-9, as added by Acts 1977, P.L. 340, §122; P.L. 336-1983, §1.]

APPENDIX C

SELECTED STATE DEFINITIONS AND PENALTIES

ALABAMA

Murder. First Degree: Perpetrated by poison lying in waiting or any other kind of willful, deliberate, malicious and premeditated killing; or committed in perpetration or attempt to perpetrate any arson, rape, robbery or burglary; or from a premeditated design unlawfully and maliciously to effect the death of any human other than one killed; or by act greatly dangerous to lives of others and evidencing a depraved mind regardless of human life.

Death or life imprisonment

Second Degree: Every other homicide, as would be murder at common law.

Not less than 10 years.

Manslaughter: First Degree: Voluntary depriving a human of life.

Second Degree: Manslaughter under any other circumstances.

Up to 1 year and up to $500.

Burglary. First Degree: In nighttime with intent to steal or commit felony, breaks and enters any inhabited dwelling or building.

Death or not less than 10 years.

Second Degree. Daytime, breaks and enters inhabited dwelling; nighttime or daytime breaks and enters uninhabitated dwelling or shop, store, etc., where goods are kept.

1 to 10 years.

Arson. First Degree: Willfully or with intent to defraud sets fire or aids in burning of dwelling.

> 2 to 10 years (death or life imprisonment if death or maiming occurs).

Second Degree: Burning of shops, store, etc. or other building or sets fire or aids burning of own property.

ALASKA

Murder. First Degree: Killing another out of deliberate and premeditated malice, or by means of poison, or in perpetrating or attempting to perpetrate rape, arson, robbery, or burglarly.

> Imprisonment at hard labor for life or for any term of years.

Second degree: Killing another purposely and maliciously.

> Not less than 15 years

Manslaughter: Unlawfully killing another.

> 1 to 20 years.

Burglary: Breaking and entering dwelling house with intent to commit crime, or armed with dangerous weapon breaks and enters, or assaults person lawfully therein.

> *1 to 10 years, up to 15 years.*
> *If human there, night or day, up to 20 years. Not dwelling house, 2 to 5 years. Breaking out of dwelling after committing, or attempting to commit crime. 1 to 3 years.*

Arson. First Degree: Willfully and maliciously setting fire to or burning or causing to be burned or aiding, counseling or procuring burning of dwelling house, whether occupied, unoccupied or vacant, or part of or belonging to adjoining dwelling, whether his property or that of another.

2 to 20 years.

Second Degree: Building not described above.

1 to 10 years.

Third Degree: Personal property of value of $100 or more.

1 to 3 years and/or find.

Fourth Degree: Attempted arson.

1 to 2 years and fine.

Defrauding insurer.

1 to 5 years and/or find.

DELAWARE

Murder: First Degree: Murder with express malice aforethought or in perpetrating, or attempting to perpetrate, rape, kidnapping, treason, etc.

Death
Second Degree: Other murders.
Life imprisonment.

Manslaughter: Not defined (except that manslaughter by husband of person found in act of adultery with wife is misdemeanor, penalty being fine of $100 to $1,000 and imprisonment up to one year).

Up to 30 years, or up to $10,000.

125

FLORIDA

Murder: First Degree: When perpetrated from a premeditated design to effect the death of the person killed or any human being, or when committed in the perpetration or attempt to perpetrate any arson, rape, robberty, or burglary.

> Death
> Second Degree: By act imminently dangerous to another, evincing a depraved mind regardless of human life, although without any premeditated design to effect the death of any particular individual.
> Life or not less than 20 years.
> Third Degree: Without any design to effect death, by a person engaged in the commission of any felony, other than arson, rape, robbery, or burglary.
> Up to 20 years.

Manslaughter: By act, procurement, or culpable negligence of another, in cases where such killings are not justifiable or excusable homicide nor murder.

> Up to 20 years or up to $5,000.

Burglary: Breaks and enters a dwelling with intent to commit a felony, or after having entered breaks such a dwelling, if armed with dangerous weapon, or with dynamite, or if assaults any person lawfully therein.

> Life imprisonment or term of years at court's discretion.
> If not armed or with explosive.
> Up to 20 years.

Burglary of buildings other than dwelling, ship or vessel.
Up to 15 years.

Arson: First Degree: Willfully and maliciously sets fire to or aids burning of any dwelling, occupied, unoccupied, or vacant property of himself or of another.
Up to 20 years.
Second Degree: Burning of any other building.
Up to 10 years.
Third Degree: Burning of personal property of value of $25 or more.
Up to 3 years.
Fourth Degree: Attempts to burn.
Up to 2 years or up to $1,000.

INDIANA

Murder: First Degree: Purposely and with premeditated malice or in the perpetration of or attempt to perpetrate a rape, arson, robbery or burglary.

Death or life imprisonment.
Second Degree: Purposely and maliciously, but without premeditation.
Life imprisonment.

Manslaughter: Voluntarily kills without malice, expressed or implied, in a sudden heat or involuntarily in the commission of some unlawful act.

2 to 21 years.

Burglary: First Degree: Breaks and enters into any dwelling with intent to commit any felony, or to do any act of violence or injury to any human being.

> 10 to 20 years.
> Second Degree: Buildings other than dwelling, boat, automobile, railroad car, etc., with intent to commit felony.
> 2 to 25 years.
> Third Degree: Any dwelling or other structure, with intent to commit misdemeanor; or enters land with intent to commit felony or severe crop or building, etc.
> Up to $500 and/or up to 1 year.

Arson: First Degree: Willfully and maliciously sets fire or aids the burning of any dwelling, occupied or unoccupied, property of another, or being insured sets fire for purpose of defrauding insurer.

> 2 to 14 years.
> Second Degree: Burning of any personal property, etc.
> 1 to 3 years.

MASSACHUSETTS

Murder: First Degree: With deliberately premeditated malice aforethought or with extreme atrocity or cruelty, or in the commission or attempted commission of a crime punishable with imprisonment for life.

> Life imprisonment.
> Second Degree: Other murders

Manslaughter: Not defined.

> Up to 20 years, or up to $1,000 fine
> and imprisonment up to 2¼ years.

Burglary: Break and enter in nighttime, dwelling, with intent to commit felony, or after entering, breaks such dwelling, any person being therein and armed with a dangerous weapon, or assaults person therein.

> Life imprisonment or term not less
> than 10 years.
> Break and enter in nighttime, dwell-
> ing, not armed, and no assault.
> 5 years and up.
> Break and enter building or ship in
> nighttime.
> Up to 20 years.
> Entering dwelling in nighttime with-
> out breaking, or breaks and enters
> building or ship in daytime.
> Up to 10 years or up to 2 years and
> up to $500.

Arson: Burning dwelling house, property of himself or another, occupied or unoccupied.

> Up to 20 years.
> Burning of other buildings.
> Up to 10 years.

MICHIGAN

Murder: First Degree: Perpetrated by means of poison, or lying in wait, or any other kind of willful, deliberate and premeditated killing, or which small be committed in the perpetration or attempt to perpetrate any arson, rape, robbery, burglary.

Life imprisonment.
Second Degree: All other kinds of murder.
Life imprisonment or term of years.
Manslaughter: Not defined.
Up to 15 years and/or up to $7500.

Burglary: Breaking and entering, with intent to commit felony, or any larceny, any dwelling or other building.

Up to 15 years.

Burglary in daytime, entering without breaking.

Up to 5 years or up to $2500.

Arson: Burning dwellinghouse, occupied, unoccupied, property of himself or another.

Up to 20 years.
Burning of other real property, other buildings.
Up to 10 years.
Burning of personal property, over $50 value.
Felony, penalty at discretion of court.
Burning of personal property, less than $50 value.
Fine or imprisonment, at discretion of court.
Burning with intent to defraud insurer.
Up to 10 years.

NEBRASKA

Murder: First Degree: Purposely and of deliberate and premeditated malice, or in the perpetration or attempt to perpetrate any rape, arson, robbery or burglary, or by administering poison, or causing the same to be done; or, by willful and corrupt perjury or subordination of the same, purposely procure the conviction and execution of any innocent person.

Death or life imprisonment.
Second Degree: Purposely and maliciously, but without deliberation and premeditation.
10 years to life.

Manslaughter: Unlawfully kill, without malice, either upon a sudden quarrel, or unintentionally, while the slayer is in commission of some unlawful act.

1 to 10 years.

Burglary: Breaks and enters dwelling, shop, office, etc., railroad car, etc., with intent to kill, rob, rape, or commit any other felony, or with intent to steal property of value.

1 to 10 years or up to $500.

In day or night, enters and attempts to kill, rob, steal, rape or commit arson, or enters armed with dangerous weapon, with intent to rob or steal and threaten to injure any person in building or with intent to rob or order any person to hand over money or property.

3 to 20 years.

Arson: First Degree: Willfully and maliciously sets fire or aids the burning of any dwelling, occupied, unoccupied or vacant, property of himself or another.

2 to 20 years.
Second Degree: Burning of other buildings or structure.

131

1 to 10 years.
Third Degree: Burning of personal property, of value of $25 or more and property of another.
1 to 3 years.
Fourth Degree: Attempts to burn.
1 to 2 years, or up to $1,000.
Burning to defraud insurer.
1 to 5 years.

NEW YORK

Murder: Acting with intent to cause death of a person, and killing that person or a third person; or, engaging recklessly, under circumstances evincing depraved indifference to human life, in conduct which creates grave risk of death to another, and in fact does cause that death; or, acting alone or with others, commits or attempt to commit robbery, burglary, kidnaping, etc., and in the course of such crime he alone or any other participant, causes death of another, not a participant.

Life imprisonment.

Manslaughter: First Degree: Acting with intent to cause serious physical injury to another person, and causing death of such person or of a third person; or, with intent to cause the death of another person, causing death under circumstances which do not constitute murder because of acting under influence of extreme emotional disturbance, mitigating circumstances reducing murder to manslaughter first degree; or, committing abortional act which is justified pursuant to 125.05 section 3 prior to July 1, 1970, or intentionally causing or aiding another person to commit suicide.

Up to 15 years.

Burglary: First Degree: With intent to commit crime, breaks and enters, in night, dwelling of another, in which there is at the time a human being, being armed with dangerous weapon, or arming inside with weapon, or assisted by confederate actually present, or while effecting entrance, or by committing crime in building, or in escaping, assaults any person.

10 to 30 years.
Second Degree: With intent to commit some crime, breaks and enters dwelling house in which there is human present, under circumstances not burglary in first degree.
Up to 15 years.
Third Degree: With intent to commit crime, breaks and enters a building, being in any building, commits crime therein, and breaks out.
Up to 10 years.

Arson: First Degree: Willfully burns in night, dwelling in where there is at the time a human being; or a car, etc., or other building, where to the knowledge of the offender, there is at the time, a human being.

Up to 40 years.
Second Degree: Commits an act of burning in daytime, which if at night, would be arson in first degree; willfully burns dwelling, in which no human being; willfully burns in nighttime, uninhabited building, but adjoining inhabited building, in which there is human, so as to

133

endanger inhabited building; willfully burns in night, car, etc., or other building, ordinarily occupied in night by human, although no person within at the time, willfully burns car, etc., or other building, which is ensured. Up to 25 years.

Third Degree: Burns personal property of another of value of $25 or over.

NORTH CAROLINA

Murder: First Degree: Perpetrated by means of poison, lying in wait, imprisonment, starving, torture or by any other kind of willful, deliberate and premeditated killing or killing committed in perpetration of, or attempt to perpetrate, arson, rape, robbery, burglary or other felony.

Death or life imprisonment.

Manslaughter: No definition.
4 months to 20 years.
Involuntary manslaughter.
Fine and/or imprisonment at discretion of Court.

Burglary: First Degree: If committed in dwelling house, and any person is in actual occupation of part of house at time of burglary.

Death or life imprisonment.
Second Degree: Committed in dwelling house, not actually occupied by anyone at time of crime.
Life imprisonment or term of years.

134

Arson: Not defined.

> Death or life imprisonment.
> Schools, public buildings.
> 5 to 10 years.
> Attempted arson.
> 4 months to 10 years.
> Punishment for other types of burn-
> ing, i.e., churches, etc.
> 20 to 40 years.

OREGON

Murder: First Degree: Purposely, and of deliberate and premeditated malice, or in the commission or attempt to commit any rape, arson, robbery or burglary.

> Life imprisonment
> Second Degree: Purposely and ma-
> liciously, but without deliberation
> and premeditation or attempt to
> commit any felony other than those
> listed above killing by act imminently
> dangerous and evincing deparvity.
> Up to 25 years.

Manslaughter: Without malice express or implied, and without deliberation, upon a sudden heat of passion, caused by a provocation apparently sufficient to make the passion irresistible, voluntarily killing; in commission of unlawful act, or lawful act without due caution or circumspection, involuntarily killing, killing by act, procurement or culpable negligence (but not murder).

> 1 to 5 years and up to $5000.

Burglary: Breaking and entering dwelling containing human being, with intent to commit crime, or having entered with such intent, breaking in nighttime a dwelling house, or armed with dangerous weapon or assaults person.

>Up to 15 years.
>Breaking and entering building, railroad car, vessel, etc.,
>Up to 10 years.
>Breaking to get out of dwelling house, in nighttime, after committing or attempting to commit crime.
>Up to 3 years.

Arson: First Degree: Willfully and maliciously setting fire or aiding burning of dwelling house, any building part of dwelling house, etc., any public building in which there is at the time a human being.

>20 years.
>Second Degree: Burning of building not in first degree category.
>10 years.
>Third Degree: Burning of property, being property of another.
>Up to 1 year.
>Attempted burning.
>Up to 3 years and/or up to $1000.

SOUTH CAROLINA

Murder: Killing of any person with malice aforethought, either express or implied.

>Death or life imprisonment.

Manslaughter: Unlawful killing of another without malice, express or implied.

2 to 30 years.
Involuntary manslaughter:
3 months to 3 years.

Burglary: As at common law.

Life or 5 years and up.
Break and enter, or break with intent
to enter, in daytime, dwelling house,
or in nighttime, with intent to commit
felony or other crime of lesser grade.
Up to 5 years.

Arson: Willfully and maliciously sets fire to or aids the burning of any dwelling, property of himself or another.

2 to 20 years.
Burning of other buildings.
1 to 10 years.
Burning of personal property to defraud insurer.
1 to 5 years.
Burning of personal property.
1 to 3 years.

TENNESSEE

Murder: Unlawfully kill any reasonable creature in being, and under the peace of the state, with malice aforethought, either express or implied.

First Degree: Perpetrated by means
of poison, lying in wait, or by any
other kind of wilful, deliberate,
malicious and premeditated killing,
or committed in the perpetration of
or attempt to perpetrate, any murder
in the first degree, arson, rape, robbery, burglary or larceny.

Death or life imprisonment.
Second Degree: All other kinds of murder.
10 to 20 years.

Manslaughter: Unlawful killing of another without malice, either voluntary upon a sudden heat, or involuntary, but in the commission of some unlawful act.

Voluntary manslaughter.
2 to 10 years.
Involuntary manslaughter.
1 to 5 years.

Burglary: Breaking and entering dwelling house by night with intent to commit felony.

5 to 15 years.
Second Degree: Breaking or entering by day, with intent to commit felony.
3 to 15 years.

Arson: Willfully and maliciously setting fire to or aiding burning of any house or building, property of himself or another.

3 to 21 years.
Attempted arson. 1 to 5 years.

TEXAS

Murder: Voluntarily killing any person.

Death or life term of years not less than 2 years.

Manslaughter: Statute repealed. Homicide by negligence instead.

First Degree: In performance of a
lawful act.
Up to 1 year or $1,000.
In performance of an unlawful act
which is misdemeanor.
Up to 3 years or up to $3,000.
In performance of unlawful act not
offense against Penal Law.
Up to 1 year and up to $1,000.

VERMONT

Murder: First Degree: Murder committed by means of
poison, lying in wait or by deliberate and premeditated
killing, or committed in perpetrating or attempting to
perpetrate arson, rape, robbery, or burglary.

Life imprisonment.

Murder of prison employee or law enforcement officer.

Death or life imprisonment as jury
determines.
Second Degree: Not defined.
Life or term as court shall

Manslaughter: Not defined.
Up to 15 years and/or $1,000.

Burglary: In nighttime, breaking
and entering dwelling, bank, shop,
store, etc., vessel, railroad car, or
other building in which personal
property is situated, with intent to
commit murder, rape, robbery,
larceny or other felony.

Up to 15 years and/or up to $1,000.

139

Burglary as above, but in daytime.
Up to 10 years or up to $1,000.

Arson: First Degree: Willfully and maliciously setting fire to or aiding burning of dwelling house, occupied, unoccupied or vacant, property of himself or another.

2 to 10 years or up to $2,000.
Death resulting-murder first degree.
Second Degree: Burning of other buildings or structures, property of himself or another.
1 to 5 years or up to $1,000.

VIRGINIA

Murder: First Degree: By poison, lying in wait, imprisonment, starving, or by any willful deliberate and premeditated killing, or killing in commission of, or attempt to commit, arson, rape, abduction, robbery or burglary.

Death or life imprisonment or not less than 20 years.
Second Degree: All other murder. 5 to 20 years.

Manslaughter: Not defined.
Voluntary Manslaughter.
1 to 5 years or up to $1,000 and/or up to 1 year.

Burglary: Breaking and entering dwelling of another in nighttime with intent to commit felony or larceny, even though thing stolen is less than $50 value.

Death or life, or not less than 5 years.

140

In night without breaking, or in daytime breaking and entering dwelling occupied, or office, shop, etc., railroad car, automobile (if used as dwelling place) etc., with intent to commit murder, rape, or robbery.
1 to 20 years.
As above, but with intent to commit larceny or other felony.
1 to 20 years, or up to 12 months and up to $1,000.
As above, but with intent to commit assault or other misdemeanor.
1 to 10 years, or up to 1 year, $1,000.

Arson: In nighttime, maliciously burning or using explosive, or aiding burning of any dwelling, property of himself or another.

Death or 5 to 20 years.
If occupied, but in daytime; or barn at night, meeting house, college, etc.
3 to 15 years, unoccupied 2 to 10 years.
Burning of other buildings, if no one present and property of value of $100 or more.
2 to 10 years.
burning to defraud insurer.
1 to 10 years.

WYOMING

Murder: First Degree: With premeditated malice and purposely or in perpetration of, or attempt to perpetrate, rape, arson, robbery, or burglary, or by poison.

Life imprisonment or death.
Second Degree: Purposely and maliciously, but without premeditation.
20 years to life.

Manslaughter: Unlawfully kills without malice, express or implied, either voluntarily, upon sudden heat of passion, or involuntarily but in commission of unlawful act or by any culpable neglect or criminal carelessness.

Up to 20 years.

INDEX

INDEX